DATE DUE

Society Against Itself

Society Against Itself

by
GEORGE H. CROWELL

THE WESTMINSTER PRESS
Philadelphia

LIBRARY OF CONGRESS CATALOG CARD No. 68–22810

Published by The Westminster Press ®
Philadelphia, Pennsylvania

PRINTED IN THE UNITED STATES OF AMERICA

TO MY WIFE, ELAINE

Contents

Preface

THIS BOOK is addressed to those who are deeply concerned about the urgent social crises of our day. It is addressed to those who are troubled by injustices in our collective life which arouse bitter hostilities among human groups, creating dangerous possibilities for destructive conflict. It is addressed especially to those who long to make significant contributions to needed social change in American society, but who are so overwhelmed and bewildered by the enormity of the problems in relation to their own feeble influence in a complex social order that they feel unable to initiate any effective social action.

This study grew out of my distress as a Christian that the churches have served far too ineffectively as instruments of desperately needed social change. Their frequent failures have been repudiations of their responsibility as bearers of the gospel which calls for vigorous response to human need of all kinds. To be sure, the churches possess a great deal of potential power for effecting needed change, and they have occasionally made creative and even heroic contributions to social justice. But such activity is exceptional. Since the churches are thoroughly integrated with the prevailing order in American society, as a considerable body of recent literature has shown (see, for example, Peter L. Berger, *The Noise of Solemn Assemblies*, Doubleday & Company, Inc., 1961), their failures are understandable. But individual Christians certainly need

11

not be confined within the institutional limitations of the
churches. They have freedom of movement and opportunity
for initiative on controversial issues rarely possessed by slow-
moving religious institutions which usually are preoccupied
with preserving internal harmony. But why have individuals,
too, so largely failed to meet the need for social action? The
difficulties that hinder Christians in American society from
mustering sufficient motivation and energy to initiate needed
social action are by no means unique to Christians. All Americans confront the same basic difficulties. The present volume,
a revision of my doctoral dissertation, is addressed, therefore,
to all who are sensitive to the urgent need for social action,
regardless of formal religious affiliation or nonaffiliation. The
injustices that plague our society affect all of us, and in countless different ways require cooperative effort from all of us.

American society is generating social problems far more
rapidly than its existing institutions can cope with them. Thus
our society works against itself. The few bold Americans who
are social activists are unable to provide sufficient initiative to
compensate for this dangerous defect in our society. Many
more activists are needed. Why are there so few? Why do we
have difficulty in providing the needed initiative?

For a key to this problem, I have turned primarily to the
insights of sociology. Although I am not a professional soci-
ologist, I am deeply appreciative of the self-understanding
with which sociology has provided us. I have attempted to
make use of its general approach and of many of its research
results in order to throw some light upon the problem of motivation for social action in our society. Since I have taken on
an issue far too large to be dealt with adequately within the
limits of these few pages, I have necessarily oversimplified
and have left untouched many relevant matters. To be sure, at
many points my more lengthy dissertation, "American Cultural
Values Obstructing Christian Social Action," which is on file
in the Library of Union Theological Seminary in New York
City, provides more thorough documentation of the views pre-

sented here. But its substantive conclusions are basically the same, and it has the same basic limitations. The present volume is not intended as an exhaustive treatment. It aims, rather, at being provocative and suggestive. It is intended to stimulate discussion. My hope is that each reader will apply my conclusions to his own situation, and will modify my judgments in the light of reality for him.

These pages have grown out of my concern that more Americans become actively involved in social action. But I am convinced that the usual denunciations of apathy and the usual exhortations that we bestir ourselves to do something about the mess in our society are quite futile. Rather, I have simply attempted to describe in considerable detail the social pressures working in American society against our initiating social action. While these pressures are not unfamiliar, most of us are probably not aware of their cumulative effect. Contemplating them can well create a deep sense of discouragement. This is hardly the response that I desire. But I have faith that a realistic recognition of these social pressures can offer possibilities for a new freedom to engage in social action.

For two summer research grants which freed me to prepare these pages, I am grateful to Lake Forest College. For painstaking work on the typescripts of both the dissertation and the present revision, my thanks go to Mrs. Helen E. Hurd.

I am indebted to Profs. Robert T. Handy and Roger L. Shinn, and especially to Profs. C. Ellis Nelson and Robert W. Lynn of the Union Theological Seminary Faculty, who provided invaluable suggestions, criticisms, support, and encouragement during the preparation of this manuscript in its earlier form as my Th.D. dissertation. Prof. Donald E. Roos of the Department of Sociology and Anthropology at Lake Forest College provided cogent comments which have helped me in preparing the present revision. I am grateful to him and to others who have given helpful suggestions. But responsibility for the views presented here is, of course, my own.

A special note of thanks is due Prof. Reinhold Niebuhr who, although in no direct way involved in the writing of this book, nevertheless helped to make it possible through his profound influence on the direction of my thinking and of my work.

G. H. C.

Lake Forest, Illinois
November, 1967

Society Against Itself

1

Social Action:
Fulfillment of Two Divergent Needs

Two QUITE DIFFERENT but extremely urgent needs press in
upon us. One is the crucial requirement for achieving justice
in our collective life and for overcoming the hostilities that
alienate human groups from one another around this troubled
world of ours. The other is the critical necessity for individuals
in the heavily populated, urbanized, industrialized, bureaucratized modern world to find their own, independent sense of
meaning in a social context that demands conformity. Those
who engage in social action can contribute at the same time
toward meeting both this pressing need in the surrounding society and this pressing need within themselves.

The Need for Social Justice

Injustices of such overwhelming complexity, of such profound depth, and with such dangerous potential consequences
confront us in our collective life that human existence as we
know and value it lies constantly under the threat of destruction. Many such injustices are so obvious that they hardly require mention. They include the explosive issue of race relations, continuing poverty amid plenty, the decay of our inner
cities, technological unemployment, the waste of natural resources, the relationship of affluent nations to poverty-stricken,
underdeveloped nations, and antagonism among nations with

the frightful consequences of war. Many other injustices, actual and potential, with all sorts of complicated relations to one another and to those already mentioned could be added.[1]

Injustices in the modern world get out of hand as they accumulate and multiply in an era of bewilderingly rapid social change. The major impetus behind the accelerating social change of our day is the accelerating pace of discovery in the sciences and the rapid translation of these discoveries into new technologies which are revolutionizing our lives. Scientific research is pursued vigorously largely because it provides extraordinarily promising possibilities for improving the conditions of human existence. For the first time in human history, thanks to modern science, the possibility that the dreaded foes of humanity—hunger, exposure, disease, and want—can be banished lies within our grasp. But the technological changes that we eagerly pursue often produce social injustices that we would gladly have avoided. Automation intensifies the agony of unemployment. Modern weapons greatly enhance the oppressive power controlled by dictators. Although the achievements of science have raised hopes among all men for escape from poverty, for the majority these hopes remain frustratingly unfulfilled and a source of explosive revolution.

Ours is a day of unprecedentedly rapid and unprecedentedly dangerous social change. The injustices that tear at the entrails of our collective life desperately need to be overcome before they bring catastrophe. Hence the need for social action is enormous and urgent.

Overcoming Social Injustices Through Social Action

Social action is any effort directed toward bringing about change in the institutions of society in order to effect some greater degree of justice and reconciliation among men.[2] Or to put it another way, social action is effort to overcome social injustice. The injustices that arise merely in interpersonal relationships do not concern us here. They are feeble problems in comparison with social injustice. Truly powerful are those injustices which have become institutionalized—those which have in particular societies become regarded as the normal and proper avenues of behavior, and which have been sanctified by tradition and custom. Backed by the sanction of the community, such injustices have deep and stubborn roots. Merely personal injustices—sometimes called crimes—have no such roots. On the contrary, they face community reproach. But where the community supports injustice and alienation among men, and even calls them just and proper, the community's resistance against efforts to bring about justice and reconciliation is very difficult to surmount. This difficult task is undertaken by social action.

Great numbers of people are needed now in American society and around the world to work toward overcoming the injustices that endanger our collective life. To be sure, we may not be able to solve our urgent social problems even if vast numbers of people should become intensely involved in social action. It is not at all certain that we have the tools or abilities even to understand our problems adequately. Moreover, we sometimes get caught in a web of injustice from which we can find no escape without creating some other form of injustice, and our only immediate choice is among varying degrees of injustice. Nor is it certain that we command the power to solve urgent social problems even when workable solutions are in sight—either because existing social organizations are inadequate for the task, or because special-group interests are too persistent, or because too few people are concerned about the problems to work toward their solution. Even if we should succeed in directing our energies toward overcoming injustices that now confront us, we can be sure that the rapid pace of change in the modern world will present us with new injustices, with which past human experience leaves us ill-equipped to deal, before we have overcome the old. Furthermore, since we can engage in social action with only limited knowledge and understanding of the consequences that will follow, even with the best intentions we run the risk of doing more harm than good. Thus, social action in the modern world is an endless, frustrating task. It is urgently needed, nevertheless.

To fail to engage in social action is to abdicate a basic human responsibility—which in short is simply the responsibility to care for one another. It is to leave to existing social forces a course of events that is pregnant with catastrophe. Indeed, it is to give tacit approval and support to that course of events. Social action is, to be sure, highly demanding, calling not only for a great deal of courage and creativity but also for tedious, protracted, exhausting effort in the midst of controversy, frequently with little success. Nevertheless, despite the difficulties and despite the strong possibility of failure, I personally must opt in favor of the active struggle for social justice. Anything less appears to me to be an open invitation to disaster. With this bias I have written these pages. I have forebodings for our future, but I cannot help also having faith that those who throw their energies into the struggle for social justice, into the enterprises of social action, could make crucial contributions toward averting catastrophe. Moreover, social action can be exhilarating and rewarding. At the same time that it responds to urgent social needs, it also offers possibilities for meeting urgent inner personal needs.

The Drive for Personal Fulfillment

Within the last few decades in Western nations, and especially in American society, a large body of literature has arisen which expresses in many ways the view that life in our affluent societies leaves much to be desired.[3] Despite all the glittering achievements of modern science and industry, and despite the unparalleled luxury and leisure of the modern era, personal life for many, even—and perhaps especially—among those

who are most privileged, is pervaded with a sense of emptiness
and meaninglessness. Our amazingly dynamic and wealthy society is seen frequently not as a blessing but as an accursed
enemy of personal fulfillment.

Increasing numbers of people, especially among the present
student generation, have come to dread the pervasive pressures that our society exerts, sometimes subtly and sometimes
blatantly, to gain conformity to its consumption-oriented, suburban, middle-class mold. They dread being caught working
at the lower levels of some great bureaucratic organization
that appropriates their energy, ingenuity, and time for purposes over which they have no control. They long to make
some unique, significant, valued contribution to the world.
They long to give expression to their own individual creativity
in such a way that it will leave the world, at least in some
small way, richer because it bears the indelible stamp of their
work. They long to make some contribution that nobody else
could make, or would make, or at least that nobody else has
yet made. They long, moreover, to make some contribution
that will genuinely help their fellowmen.

Often these longings are vaguely conceived and ill-defined.
Many college students today, for example, have a vague sense
of dissatisfaction with the prospect of working in bureaucratic
organizations and living in suburbia, and yet feel strongly at-
tracted by the security, the luxury, and the graciousness of
affluent, middle-class American life. Many have a foreboding
that they will ultimately be caught up in the system, and in a
vague way that they cannot fully explain, they resent this fact.
Others are able to express quite articulately, as many "hippies"
do, their dissatisfaction with major elements of American society, but are unable to arrive at a fully satisfying alternative.
Able only to rebel, they are still bound to the system against
which they rebel. But however vague and unresolved these
longings for fulfillment are, they represent in my judgment a
valid protest against our social system. We must welcome
these stirrings, and must be grateful for their witness that the

human spirit struggles so persistently to find and to fulfill itself.

It might be argued that we have ample opportunity to exercise our creativity in American society. After all, there are probably no established roles in our society in which one could not find some degree of freedom to express his own individual creativity. In the occupational world, to be sure, one is not likely to have much freedom without considerable education. The freedom for creative individual contributions would certainly be slight for those confined to highly repetitive operations on assembly lines. Nevertheless, there is almost always some room, however routine the job, for people to exercise creativity, if not in the production process itself, then in relating themselves to their fellow workers and to the public —attempting to bring human warmth and concern into relationships that might otherwise remain coldly impersonal. Moreover, many jobs—in skilled crafts, in the professions, in business management, and in scientific research—require the exercise of much talent and ingenuity. But while individual creativity may be expressed through almost any established social role, the longing for fulfillment may remain unsatisfied even among those with great freedom for creative activity. Why should this be?

The need for creative self-expression is apparently very great. Those who must perform repetitive assembly-line tasks suffer because they are cut off from a major avenue toward human fulfillment. But evidently creative activity in itself is not likely to be fully satisfying unless it also serves to meet genuine human needs. The advertising copywriter may have considerable scope to exercise creative ingenuity, but if he is simply attempting to attract public attention to a detergent with no obvious advantage over dozens of others, he may well question the value of his efforts. He may well be burdened with a sense of emptiness. The experience of fulfillment apparently results from the meeting of two vital requirements: a person must exercise his own creativity and his activity must genuinely help other human beings.[4]

It is hard to say which of these is more important. One can tolerate a great deal of drudgery—as the housewife does—if one knows that one's activity is meeting vital human needs. But meeting vital human needs may not bring satisfaction— as it fails to do with many housewives—unless one also finds outlets for truly creative self-expression. I suspect that the Peace Corps and VISTA evoke an eager response from young people today because they offer promise of meeting both these requirements for personal fulfillment.

There are, to be sure, many established social roles in our society that offer opportunities both for creative activity and for helping others but still leave a sense of incomplete fulfillment among those who participate in the restless dissatisfaction of our day. This may indicate, of course, simply a neurotic inability to be satisfied with anything. But it may also be a legitimate, constructive reluctance to become committed to the prevailing values in our society. To be satisfied with unquestioning performance of accepted roles may well be to give tacit approval to injustices institutionalized in the society. If we are to maximize both our creativity and our helpfulness, we must raise critical questions about the contributions we make through our roles in society, and we must try to exert some influence over the use to which our efforts are put.

It is not enough to respond merely to the needs of individual persons. One can express quite creatively a concern for individuals wherever one has personal contact with others, and yet experience only a partial sense of fulfillment. A person may make a valuable contribution, for example, by tutoring an underprivileged child. But he may remain dissatisfied with his contribution when the social causes of the child's deprivation remain untouched. To be sure, we would do wrongly if we failed to take satisfaction in the very real personal help that we do provide. Yet at the same time, when urgent social needs remain unaffected by this personal help, we do well to feel dissatisfied. We do well to feel profoundly dissatisfied!

Personal Fulfillment Through Social Action

Dissatisfaction with a society that institutionalizes injustices is in itself healthy and potentially creative. It can have unhealthy consequences, however. Those who respond passively to the situation, convinced that they are powerless to initiate any meaningful changes, may develop a sense of alienation that undermines their self-confidence and thus their ability to create and to love. Were they to respond to their sense of dissatisfaction by moving into social action, however, they might transform this liability of their situation into a personal asset.

Engaging in social action offers possibilities for avoiding the sense of alienation which pervades so much of American society and for gaining a sense of personal fulfillment. Whereas the sense of fulfillment experienced by the creative artist—whether poet, novelist, playwright, composer, painter, sculptor, or performing artist—requires special talent possessed by very few people, this is not true of social action. Few people lack the abilities needed for making important contributions in social action. Although special knowledge and talents may be very useful, they are not prerequisites. But those who engage in social action can find plenty of freedom to exercise their creativity, their initiative, and their sensitivity to the needs of others. They cannot expect to experience the sense of quiet, restful well-being that comes from the knowledge that all is as it ought to be. But they can experience a sense of participation in activities of vital importance for the lives of men. They can be where the action is! They can feel alive!

Engaging in social action providentially can meet two vital human needs: the need for justice in our collective life and the need for fulfillment in our personal lives. Why, then, are so few people engaged in social action?

2

Social Pressures
Against Needed Social Action

IT IS OBVIOUS that commitment to social action in American society falls far short of the need. Even as I write these words, riots of enormous scope and violence have been breaking out with increasing rapidity in a succession of our nation's inner-city ghettos, whose people are venting their fury against the racial tyranny that has kept them in bondage for more than a century since the abolition of slavery. Not only does our society need the efforts of many times the numbers of those now engaged in social action on the race problem, but it also needs untold additional numbers to work on other social problems that have not yet reached such crisis proportions. Why is the response to so many urgent needs so meager? Why indeed, since those responding would serve not only society but their own highest needs as well?

The Complexity of Social Injustices

First, it is surely obvious that almost any social injustice conspicuous enough to gain public recognition possesses endless complexities. The victims of the injustice are likely to be caught in an intricate web of suffering from which it is extremely difficult, even with a great deal of outside help, to escape. If a concerned person has enough interest in such a problem to inform himself in some detail about it, he may well experience a profound sense of discouragement about the possibility of doing anything to help remedy it before he even mobilizes enough energy to begin.

Take, for example, the problem of racial injustice. Although the complexities of this problem are familiar enough, a review of them can still be overwhelming. The Negro suffers in American society from two great handicaps intricately related to each other: his color and his poverty. Because of his color, he has been barred countless times from opportunities that whites enjoy as a matter of course in employment, in education, in housing, in medical care, in public accommodations, and in the sharing of political power. As a result, his average annual income is little more than half that of whites, and this proportion has been declining. Because of his poverty, he is severely handicapped in his struggle for political power and in his attempts to gain a decent education, both of which might help him to gain better employment, which could help him to escape poverty. Meanwhile, automation has increased his difficulty in obtaining employment by destroying jobs available to the least educated and to the least skilled. White society confines him to overcrowded ghettos with exorbitant rents for run-down, rat-infested dwellings, with dismal neighborhood schools, and with stores charging excessive prices for shoddy goods. He grows up surrounded by broken homes, drug addiction, crime, and frequently, police brutality. As a result of all that he suffers, he becomes so profoundly discouraged that when opportunities do become available to him, he is often unable even to recognize them.[1]

How can the concerned person, white or black, who would like to help overcome this vast network of injustice do anything sufficiently effective to help? Many, without sufficient recognition of the depth and difficulty of the problem, have dabbled in attempts to help and, upon suffering defeat, have felt rudely rebuffed. In the face of complex social injustices like the race problem, discouragement comes easily.

The Feeling of Powerlessness

Even if one is not daunted by the complexity of social injustices, he may be discouraged from engaging in social action by his insufficient control over political power, or by what he feels to be insufficient access to such power. Great numbers of people in American society are infected with a deep sense of powerlessness and uselessness. Even among the more privileged, who are well educated and who fill important positions for which they receive high income, this feeling of powerlessness prevails. As C. Wright Mills points out, the individual in our mass society, with its huge political and economic organizations, is left with a sense of powerlessness that leads to "the most profound apathy of modern times."[2]

The individual may value highly his right to vote, but he is not easily convinced that his lone vote among many thousands or millions of others carries any real weight. Surely very few Americans feel that they exercise any meaningful influence over decisions made by our national government, especially on matters of foreign policy. Few enough feel that they are able to exercise influence over affairs in even their own local communities. Even those with a strong desire to work in social action can well become discouraged before they begin, not only by the complexity of social injustices, but also by the mystery and obscurity in the workings of political power and by their sense of distance from the centers of power.

There is good reason for this widespread feeling of powerlessness, even with regard to local issues. During recent years numerous empirical studies of power structure in various American communities have been produced. Not only have these revealed a complex pattern of power in each individual situation, but also, in their inability to agree either on the nature of community power or on a satisfactory research method, they have further testified to the great complexity of the matter.[3] If social scientists with their elaborate research programs have difficulty in understanding the structure of power in American communities, how is the layman to fare? In general these studies show that, in most American communities, power is likely to be concentrated in the hands of relatively few key persons, who very frequently are not among the elected or appointed public officials. Therefore, the lines of power and control are often hidden from the public. And yet rarely is the possibility for exercising influence for social change readily accessible to those outside the centers of power.

The power realities of American community life offer major obstacles not only to the enterprise of social action but also to the motivation and interest that are essential in order to propel people into social action. These power realities confront anyone who entertains the prospect of launching out on social action, and they may well prevent many people from even entertaining the prospect.

A Matter of Commitment

How crucial are these two factors as obstacles to motivation for social action? Are they adequate to explain the meager commitment to social action in our society? To be sure, it is discouraging that social injustices are so terribly complex and that those who do not already hold positions of power have great difficulty in initiating social changes. But the fact of the matter is that a commonsense approach that is really quite simple serves to overcome both these difficulties. Anyone who is able to employ this approach or something approximating it can initiate social action.

To begin with, if an individual is intensely concerned about some broad social problem like racial injustice, he must first focus his attention on some limited aspect of the problem that is in some way within his reach. For example, a resident of an all-white suburb might decide to work toward overcoming housing segregation in his community. He must make up his mind that he is willing to work at this single issue with great persistence over a long period of time. It will be apparent in nearly all cases that he cannot proceed very far without the help of others. But, having made his own commitment, he can then proceed to find a few other people who share his concern and who are willing to make the same sort of commitment to work with him on this single issue. Initially, one other deeply committed person may be enough. Together they can study the problem and decide on their strategy for starting action. As they gain momentum, providing each other mutual support and stimulus, they will find other concerned individuals and groups upon whom they can rely for assistance, and they will increasingly come to discern the power channels through which they must work. They may establish a formal organization to work toward their goal, but they, as the small core of committed individuals which may add or drop a member occasionally, will still provide the real momentum. If they are able to maintain their commitment and drive, they can expect to make significant, if small, contributions to needed social change. Perhaps, as an unexpected consequence, they might even achieve dramatic changes. But even if their achievements are small, they can experience the exhilaration of creative struggle for some increased measure of justice among their fellow-men.

This is a very simple procedure. But obviously it is not so simple in our society. It calls for a depth of commitment to consistent, demanding work over a long period of time that is not easily gained for social action. Surely this is not simply because social action—given the complexity of social injustices and the difficulty of gaining access to power—is hard work. There are a great many other things for which Americans are quite willing to work fully as hard as social action requires, against equally great obstacles, and with no greater assurance of success.

The real discouragement comes not from the external difficulties that social action must overcome but from the values we hold which fail to give social action the priority it needs. Our values are not nearly so much the result of our own independent thinking as we who pride ourselves on our liberal education like to tell ourselves. They are primarily, perhaps almost entirely, a reflection of values prevailing in our culture. The meager commitment to social action in our society cannot be explained without reference to American cultural values.

The fact is that we Americans can initiate social action if we will. But we tend to feel that we are powerless to do so. The complexities of social injustices and the realities of power in our society are not enough to account for our sense of powerlessness. We are likely to be consciously aware of the discouragement that these external factors cause us, and we are likely to blame them if we happen to feel uneasy about our inaction in the face of urgent social injustices. But we are not likely to be conscious that our discouragement is supplemented by the cultural values which tend to slip past our awareness while they nevertheless profoundly influence our outlook on life. My major purpose in these pages is to describe the way in which the value system that is embedded in American culture obstructs the development of attitudes that would provide impulses toward social action. Conscious awareness of these values may weaken their influence over us.

The Thesis: Social Action Is Merely Voluntary

It is my thesis that people in the United States have great difficulty in mustering sufficient concern or interest or motivation or energy to initiate and to sustain needed social action largely because American culture, whose pervasive influence is inescapable, defines nearly all activities that contribute to the very difficult and demanding task of social action as merely voluntary. Conversely, those activities which are obligatory in American culture, especially the requirements to perform faithfully at the job and in the family, lend powerful support to the existing order.

To be sure, American ideology sometimes has a good deal to *say*, in sermons, in newspaper editorials, in public school civics classes, and in the oratory dispensed on national holidays, about the responsibility of citizens to work for improvements in their communities. But in the structure of our ongoing daily life, about which little need be said to maintain its effectiveness because it is taken for granted (although explicit legal enactments strongly buttress this order), there is in reality very little room for the impulse toward social action. Not that social action is forbidden. Rather, it tends to be squeezed out by the pressure of obligations and interests that work against social change. Performing a primary role in buttressing the existing order are job and family obligations.

Fulfillment of these obligations, which are often burdensome and unpleasant, is successfully exacted because they are so closely integrated with a system of social control which includes powerful incentives and severe penalties. Social action, which is no less demanding than a great many of the most burdensome of job or family obligations, is not integrated with any such system of social control. Therefore, impulses toward social action in our society, however essential, remain haphazard and undependable.

There are available in American society two fundamental channels through which social action can be carried out. One is the job and the other is the voluntary association. The voluntary nature of social action holds, with rare exceptions, whether it be carried on through the job or through the voluntary association. Since social action is almost always voluntary in American society, it lacks the powerful impulse that is provided to those activities which the culture defines as obligatory.

3

The Existing Order

THE HEALTH of American society requires that constant effort be directed toward social action in order that dangerous social injustices might be overcome. Unfortunately, however, the advocates of social action are placed at a great disadvantage by the very society that so urgently needs their services. There is very little binding social pressure—very little really effective pressure from within the structure of the social system itself—requiring participation in activity directed toward social action, which is left to voluntary initiative. Fortunately our social system does not leave all vital matters optional—as no functioning system can. Daily work for the necessities of life is not a matter of choice. Nor is the upbringing and support of children by their parents a matter of option. We can be grateful that these and other important matters are institutionalized obligations for which our social system provides powerful incentives, and which we shirk only at the peril of an active disapproval from the community. In many ways, our society enables us to be a good deal more responsible than most of us could be without its control. Yet it does very little to encourage us to be responsible for social action. Unfortunately, social action, which involves challenging and changing the existing social order, is not an institutionalized obligation. Our society exerts its main energies in protecting and in preserving the existing order. The lives of Americans are so ordered within the American social system that they are required to fulfill obligations, notably in their jobs and in their families, which primarily—indeed overwhelmingly—support the existing order. Let us consider in more specific detail the nature of this existing order which we are obliged to support, and which we may, in our spare time, work to change if we feel so inclined.

Power in the Existing Order

The existing order is, to be sure, not simply static and resistant to change.[1] Certain types of change, resulting primarily from research in science and from innovation in industry, are an institutionalized part of the American social system. But our social system strongly resists other types of change. It resists change in the prevailing occupational system, in the prevailing status system, in the prevailing arrangements of power. Indeed, American society can be characterized as a system of power arranged so that it protects the existing order (provided, of course, that we include within this "existing order" whatever types of change it permits and promotes).[2] Within this order are established who has privilege and status, and by what means these are attained in the society, and who has legitimate power to make decisions affecting others, and by what means.

That there are particularly privileged and powerful groups in the society is not essentially the result of any conscious conspiracy on the part of these groups. The form that our social system has taken is well beyond the control or intention of any individual or group. It is a fortuitous—or providential—confluence of geography, of climate, of upheavals natural and human, and of the aspirations, strivings, decisions, and activities of many, many people, in other lands as well as in our own, over a very long period of history. Our social order has in large part unconsciously developed a style of life determined by any particular individual only in the minutest degree. Yet it influences each of us to an enormous extent. It influences the privileged and the powerful about as much as it influences anyone else, if not more. To be sure, many privileged and powerful people consciously strive and connive to preserve their privilege and power. But the culture is not the result of a conspiracy of power. Rather, it sets the conditions within which individuals can successfully conspire to gain or to maintain privilege and power.

Most of those who occupy positions of power are probably a good deal less independent of the culture than are some others who have considerably less power. Their power to make decisions for others is derived from established social roles in which they happen to be serving. They are granted the power and privilege of serving in such roles largely because they have demonstrated in their occupational life that they are faithful supporters of the existing order. Only in a limited sense do they exercise personal control over their fellow citizens. In a more basic sense, they merely exercise (more or less efficiently) the power given them by the role they play within the total social system of which they are a part. They have very little to say concerning the purpose that their exercise of power serves. This has already been determined by the culture. The personal self-interest of the powerful—the very content of which almost invariably reflects their overwhelming acceptance of the culture's prevailing values—makes them guardians of the existing order. Indeed, it could be said that the culture employs them as its instruments par excellence for maintaining the existing order.

A top executive in a large corporation, for example, is in a position to make decisions having far-reaching impact on the welfare of his fellow citizens. He can profoundly influence consumption habits. The employment or unemployment of many thousands rests in his hands. But he has very little control over the fact that our society is committed more to the manufacture of consumer durable goods than it is to raising tax money for water conservation or for public recreation areas, or indeed for almost any other purpose requiring public rather than private expenditure.[3] If his company profits from this fact, he will do all in his power to promote the public appetite for consumer durables, and possibly also the public aversion to taxes. This is his role. There is little he could do—even if he wanted to—to revise it. If he fails to play it well, he will be replaced. He takes advantage of the public desire for consumer durable goods, but he did not create it. This desire has grown out of a long cultural development to which millions have contributed and to which no individual has contributed more than the minutest amount. All the frenzied consumers of consumer durables contribute to frenzied production of these goods. Each one's appetite for them feeds the appetites of others. But even the outstanding figures in the development of this desire, such as Henry Ford and his family, have only barely influenced it. It is more accurate to say that they have been extraordinarily astute in gaining personal renown and fortune by stepping in tune with the existing trend. All of us are caught up in a social system over which we have very little control.

Americans who occupy positions of power seem to enjoy exercising their power. Yet they commonly disclaim the fact that they possess or that they seek power.[4] Perhaps this is true not merely because they can more easily maintain their power by calling as little attention to it as possible, but also because they are really not conscious of acting as independent decision makers. Perhaps their reticence reflects an unconscious honesty, for surely they are not independent decision makers. They are working for ends that have been determined for them by the cultural milieu in which they have grown up and in which they have found a prominent place.

The pages of this book are largely devoted to a description of power in American society. But they are not primarily concerned with the exercise of power for consciously determined ends. Rather, these pages are concerned with the power of social arrangements, accepted unconsciously and taken for granted, which regulate our lives at every point although we are scarcely aware of their power over us. They are concerned with the way in which Americans take on roles whereby they become instruments of power for ends that they themselves have not determined, and of which they may be only dimly aware, even when they give explicit, rational justification for these ends. In short, these pages will show how American culture, with its pervasive power, effectively undermines the impulse toward social action especially because it gains control over us in ways of which we are generally unaware.

The Fundamental Obligations in American Society

Voluntary activity in our society, including social action, is placed at a profound disadvantage in comparison with obligatory activity because it has to settle for what is left over of people's time and energy after they have fulfilled their obligations, and because the cultural means of motivation that are present in the social system strongly favor obligatory activity. To be sure, some types of voluntary activity draw strength from the system of motivation and control by which the cultural obligations are enforced because they are extensions of these obligations and closely support them. Social action, however, is not among these types.

There are two fundamental, virtually inescapable, personal obligations that have a vital bearing on social action. These are the obligations to the job and to the family. Law and custom provide powerful sanctions to ensure the faithful performance of these obligations, because such performance by the great bulk of our population is essential for the functioning of our social system. To be sure, continuous social action, as I have pointed out above, is also essential for the functioning of our social system, and yet there is very inadequate provision for the impulse toward social action in our society. Why should our society make adequate provision to ensure performance of job and family obligations but not to ensure the performance of necessary social action? The reason lies in the fact that the former are immediate needs whereas the latter is postponable. The performance of job and family obligations is an urgent, short-range, day-to-day consideration that cannot be neglected without immediate, disruptive consequences. But social action is a long-range consideration that can usually be postponed without immediate, obvious repercussions.

There are, certainly, in addition to these two major obligations, many others. Some grow directly out of the major obligations. Especially prominent among these is the requirement that children attend school, which is essential for their obtaining most jobs. Many other obligations, however, are relatively independent of the job and of the family. Among these are written laws having to do with traffic regulation, city zoning, civil rights, taxes, the draft, and many other matters. Although some of these have great importance, they are (except for military service in wartime) not nearly as dominant in the life of the individual as are job and family obligations.

These personal obligations as set by American culture exercise virtually inescapable power over the individual. They direct his activity into channels that primarily maintain and support the existing order, and that generally obstruct any impulse toward social action. Their power derives largely from the fact that they are closely integrated with the leading structural features of our social system. These leading features are the economic and the political orders. Economic and political factors shape our contemporary lives and history more than any other elements in our society.[5] To be sure, they are not free from influence by other components of our social system. Rather, they interact with each other and with these other components—notably the kinship system, the great network of voluntary associations, the status system, and the religious beliefs and institutions—in ways that are extremely complicated and have thus far eluded any complete, systematic description in sociological terms. Nevertheless, it seems reasonably safe to state that our economic and political orders generally shape the other components of our social system much more than the others shape them.

An integral part of the economic and of the political orders is our occupational system. The jobs that people hold and the daily work that they do for pay are obviously indispensable for the functioning of these orders. Therefore, the obligation to work in some job or occupation takes precedence over all other personal obligations (except in time of national emergency).[6] The obligation to the family, although indispensable to our society and very difficult for the married individual to evade, so fits into the structure of the American social system that it is clearly subordinate to the obligation to perform faithfully in the job. The family has been so shaped and fitted into the American social system that it eminently serves the needs of our occupational system, both directly and indirectly. It does so directly by facilitating the flow of workers to those points in our occupational system where they are most vitally needed. It does so indirectly by helping to prepare children for participation in the world of occupation, and by helping to provide adults with emotional gratification and fulfillment that are not available on the job. The family is not strategically enough located in our society that it can serve as an independent channel for the expression of social action. Since it is so well adapted to serving the needs of the occupational system, the obligation to the family buttresses the job obligation in supporting and in preserving the existing order.

In intricate ways, job and family obligations are closely inter-related. Our occupational system would soon be disrupted if people failed to fulfill their family obligations. By the same token, the family system would soon be disrupted if people failed to fulfill their job obligations. Each one is dependent upon the other. Each one reinforces the other. Thus the combined impact of these two interlocking obligations greatly increases the power of the other in inhibiting social action. Moreover, just as our family system, along with other features of our social system, buttresses the occupational system, so also do a great many additional social arrangements buttress the prevailing family system—thus giving further assurance of its fulfilling functions required by the occupational system.

Primary Obligation: The Job

Only at the beginning and at the end of life when one is not capable of working—or is deemed not capable—does one enjoy immunity from the primary obligation to render faithful service in some job or occupation. Children in school are preparing for participation in the world of occupation, and women in the home provide backing, support, and a base of operations for the working men and for the schoolchildren. While in any individual case a man may engage in a work through concern more for his family than for his job, yet in our total social system, the obligation to the family is subordinated to the obligation to perform faithfully in the job.[7]

Occupation is the pacesetter in the life of the individual in American society. As the Lynds put it in their second study of Middletown, a fairly typical small American city:

One's job is the watershed down which the rest of one's life tends to flow in Middletown. Who one is, whom one knows, how one lives, what one aspires to be,—these and many other urgent realities of living are patterned for one by what one does to get a living and the amount of living this allows one to buy.[8]

Perhaps the priority of occupation seems all too obvious. It appears to be rooted in the economic necessities of life. Men must obviously work in order to survive, or at least some must work in order to keep the others alive. However, even in cultures where all are expected to contribute their share of work, one's obligation to work is not necessarily regarded as primary. One of the most obvious alternative possibilities for prior obligation as defined by a culture is the demand for loyalty to the

extended family. In such a culture, the requirements for work
are subordinated to the kinship system, as in Chinese society,
at least of the precommunist era.[9] Loyalty to the family is like-
wise the primary requirement of Hebrew culture as described
in the Bible.[10]

Evidence for this contrast between the priority of family obligations as seen in Hebrew culture and the priority of job obligations as seen in American culture can be observed very
clearly in the differing ways in which each of these cultures answers the question of who a man is. When confronted with the
question, "Who is Saul?" the Biblical writer answers by saying
that he is the son of "Kish, the son of Abiel, son of Zeror, son of
Becorath, son of Aphiah, a Benjaminite" (I Sam. 9:1). But in
our society today, when confronted with the question, for example, "Who is Joseph C. Wilson?" we feel that the proper answer, the really informative answer, is, "He is the chairman
of the Board of Directors of Xerox Corporation." Mr. Wilson's
occupation is known almost everywhere his name is known,
but very few people who know this know his father's name,
much less his grandfather's. Men in our society are identified
primarily by their jobs. In the case of the married woman or
the child, we do not feel that we have adequately identified
them unless we know the occupation of their husband or
father.

Secondary Obligation: The Family

The dominant kinship pattern in the United States is the
nuclear or conjugal family. The typical nuclear family in our
society, consisting of parents and their children, is closely knit
together not only by ties of blood and affection but also by a
common status derived primarily from the occupation of the
husband-father, by pooled economic resources, and by maintenance of a single household normally separate from any rela-

tives. The nuclear family is largely isolated from wider kinship connections. Thus mutual obligations between the nuclear family and other kin are rather tenuous, although there are all sorts of informal patterns of assistance and cooperation. In some agricultural areas, among certain ethnic groups, and among some upper-class people who are especially concerned about their lineage, there is greater than normal emphasis on the extended family. Lower-class, "mother-centered" families are another kind of exception to the norm. But in general, the nuclear family, largely isolated from wider kinship connections, predominates in American society, especially in the great middle class.[11]

The individual who marries is a member of two nuclear families: that into which he was born, the family of orientation, and that which comes into being through his marriage, the family of procreation. Each of these nuclear families plays a crucial role in the life of the individual. The family of orientation vitally affects the formation of his personality The family of procreation demands of him a high degree of personal commitment and a large proportion of his time and energy. The individual's obligations to his family of procreation are obviously far more demanding than his obligations to his family of orientation. Parents generally expect their children to grow up to independence of their family of orientation and into their own occupational and parental roles. In some cases, of course, the needs of aging parents can place heavy demands upon their adult children. But, in general, the weight of family responsibility comes most heavily with marriage and parenthood. Thus, when dealing with obligations to the family, I shall be referring mainly to the family of procreation. Once a person marries, his primary family loyalty shifts to his family of procreation. Indeed, if this were not so, the nuclear family system would not be possible. And it is this nuclear family system which is so admirably adapted to serving the needs of our occupational system.

Support from the Nuclear Family
for the Occupational System

In our industrialized, urbanized, technical society, characterized by large bureaucratic organizations in both the economic
and the political orders, there is need for a highly mobile work
force. Workers must be able to move geographically with the
shifting fortunes of our economic system, and with the shifting
responsibilities of governmental agencies. Young executives in
large corporations with far-flung bases of operations are especially likely to be shifted from one place to another, where their
training, competence, and experience can be best used by their
companies.[12] The nuclear family is a small enough unit that it
has a ready mobility that the older European pattern of the extended family, with its larger size and with its tendency to be
anchored by property and tradition to a particular locality,
lacked.

Our occupational system also needs personnel for a bewil-
dering variety of jobs. An increasing number of these require a
high degree of training. With rapid advances in science and in
technology, new kinds of work requiring new skills and training are constantly appearing. Thus there is need for a labor
force free to respond to ever-new demands for talent, skill, and
training.[13] The extended family system, with its accompanying
tendency toward traditionally prescribed occupational roles,
does not allow the individual sufficient flexibility so that the
needs of our occupational system can be met. The nuclear family system, however, is not bound by such traditions. In per-
mitting a high degree of freedom in the choice of occupations,
it ensures the availability of workers for new types of jobs.

Not only geographical mobility and flexibility in the choice
of work but also social mobility is required by our occupational system. With the great emphasis that our society places
on technical efficiency, there is a pressing need for competent,
experienced leadership talent both in government and in in-

dustry. High income and status are available to those who are able and willing to take on the burdens and responsibilities involved in managerial positions. The nuclear family pattern in our society is compatible with recruitment of leadership talent from all classes, and with the granting of status on the basis of actual achievement in the world of occupation. There are, to be sure, all sorts of obstacles to social mobility in the United States. But the nuclear family pattern permits and encourages such mobility whereas the extended family pattern, in which status is generally ascribed at birth, makes such mobility very difficult. The nuclear family system allows for changes in status from one generation to another, and even within the career of one man. The young executive with his nuclear family is able to move to the more prestigious neighborhood and social club as he rises in his company.[14]

Not only in these fairly direct ways does the family support the occupational system, but it also does so in more indirect ways. It serves the occupational system by performing indispensable functions in behalf of the members of the society who presently and potentially make up the work force. In the normal case, it provides for the birth and upbringing of children, giving them their closest and most dependable human relationships during their most dependent years. At the same time, the nuclear family serves as the primary instrument in the socialization of children—doing much to prepare them for full adult participation in society, a primary component of which is, of course, the occupational system. For the husband-father, life in the nuclear family offers possibilities for personal fulfillment, enrichment, and gratification that are not available elsewhere. The sense of fulfillment he gains with his family can provide him with emotional support which helps him to perform more effectively in his job.

The nuclear family is rather well adapted for standing the strains resulting from competition for status in the world of occupation. An important element in the nuclear family system, which contributes to its stability, is the differentiated roles played by husband and wife. Although increasing numbers of women are taking employment outside the home, the role of housewife remains overwhelmingly predominant for women with small children. In the occupational world women seldom compete on an equal footing with men because their jobs are generally of lesser status or of a different type from the jobs held by men.[15] Thus, whether the married woman works or remains a housewife, there is seldom any danger of her disrupting family solidarity by competing with her husband as the chief provider of income and status for the family.[16] Further, although sharp differences in status among the male members of the extended family could be disruptive, under the nuclear family system fathers and sons or brothers can gain quite different occupational statuses without seriously disrupting their essential family life—that of their own nuclear or conjugal families.[17]

There is still another indirect way by which the nuclear family bolsters our occupational system. The achievement orientation of the occupational system is both reflected and reinforced in the fact that choosing a mate, setting up a home, and rearing a family are regarded as achievements.[18] This would not be likely to be so regarded under a system of arranged marriages, where relationships to the extended family are more important than the marriage bond. Our occupational system, which relies heavily upon the practice of granting status for achievement won in competition with others, gains strength—in ways, to be sure, that are difficult to measure—when achievement is emphasized in other elements of our social system, as it is in the family.[19]

Social Arrangements
Buttressing the American Family System

In addition to these more or less indirect ways by which the nuclear family pattern supports the occupational system, there are various social arrangements that even less directly support the occupational system because they buttress the nuclear family. For example, the relative independence of the nuclear family is reinforced in our patterns of courtship, marriage, and divorce. Young people are granted considerable freedom and initiative in the selection of marriage partners. Thus strong mutual attraction is considered essential for initiation and preservation of the marriage bond, and romantic love is fostered and encouraged.[20] To be sure, there is strain in the nuclear family system at precisely this point. The marriage bond depends very heavily upon the husband-wife relationship since there are ordinarily no comparably close ties with any other family members through which emotional support can be gained by the marriage partners. They are thrown very much upon each other. Many marriages crack under the strain, as statistics indicating the increase in divorce in the United States testify. There has been a tendency toward liberalization of divorce laws in recent years. Our divorce laws and customs, however, are not a cause of strain, but, rather, have developed as a means of coping with the strain. Despite the increase in divorce, there is no real evidence that the institution of the nuclear family is disintegrating. On the contrary, the proportion of the population married and living with their spouses is greater today than ever.[21]

The nuclear family system is further buttressed by arrangements for the unmarried, for the aged, and for the handicapped. Housing facilities are available in nearly every community for unmarried men and women and for elderly people in apartments, rooming houses, and hotels. The Social Security system, with old-age and survivors insurance and the old-age assistance programs, do much to provide for the aged and to help them to remain independent of their children. This purpose is also served by an increasing number of homes for the care of the aged. All sorts of agencies, public and private, have sprung up during the last few decades to provide help for children and adults with nearly every conceivable variety of handicap, physical or mental. Thus the nuclear family is spared part of the burden of problems that could be very difficult for it to bear. Still other social arrangements have developed which protect the family from the full weight of burdens resulting from unpredictable accident or illness. Industrial accident insurance, unemployment compensation, and numerous private health insurance programs have during recent years become solidly entrenched in the American social system. All these arrangements help to ensure the stability, unity, and independence of the nuclear family.[22] Since the nuclear family system so consistently supports the occupational system, so also do these various arrangements which buttress the nuclear family.

Enforcement of Job and Family Obligations

Although some Americans fail to fulfill their culturally prescribed obligations, most of them perform quite faithfully at their jobs and in their families. This is an impressive achievement for the American social system, especially in the case of the job, since a large proportion of the working population finds little joy in its work. To be sure, those with greater education or skill are a good deal more likely to find work that they enjoy. In a nationwide poll, 85 percent of the professionals indicated interest and enjoyment in their work. But 64 percent of white-collar and only 41 percent of factory workers so indicated.[23] C. Wright Mills points out that modern work, especially at the lower levels of bureaucratic organizations and on factory assembly lines, is basically unpleasant for most people. There is too little possibility, for example, for the craftsman's pride in skillful, creative activity. Much of the satisfaction with work that was expressed in the poll was probably not so much an indication of enjoyment of the work for its own sake as it was satisfaction with the income, or status, or power derived from work, as well as the leisure into which one can escape from the world of work and which can be made more pleasant by one's earnings from work.[24] In view of the considerable dissatisfaction with work in our society, it is apparent that rather powerful instruments of social control are necessary to ensure fulfillment of the primary obligation to work.

There are two fundamental instruments of social control by which the job obligation is enforced. First, daily work at the job is the primary source of income for most Americans. Second, the job is the primary source of status in American society. These two means of social control are intimately and intricately related to each other, mainly because income is an important indicator of status in our society, but also because status can indirectly become a source of income. Both income and status are sources of power, which, if gained in sufficient degree, can further enhance income and status. Able to grant or to deny these crucial needs, our society exerts enormous pressure to ensure faithful performance in the job.

The instruments of social control enforcing the job obligation are strongly reinforced by the demands of the family. The possibility of a man's fulfilling his obligation to his family usually depends upon his holding a job. There is pressure upon him to hold a job not only in order to support his family financially but also to help maintain its status. Even a man who is willing to risk his job on his own account—as might well be necessary if he engaged in social action—would probably be reluctant to risk the security, comfort, and status of his family as well. It is my guess that most people receive more personal gratification in their family life than in their work.[25] If this is true, it is not a serious drawback for our occupational system, since most families' income is derived primarily from earnings on the job. Concern for the welfare of his family is unquestionably a powerful impulse toward faithful performance on the job, even for a person who does not enjoy his work.

It is clear how the obligation to the job is enforced. But what of the obligation to the family? Here the case is not so clear because we are not constrained to fulfill the family obligation in the obvious, inescapable manner that we are compelled to fulfill the job obligation. Our social system relies more upon incentives and inducements to encourage faithfulness in the family than it does upon threats and penalties to discourage unfaithfulness. In marriage, which offers socially approved opportunities for expression of sexual drives, the threat of loneliness can be largely overcome, and each partner can gain needed emotional support through the appreciation and understanding he receives from the other. In parenthood, husband and wife can be drawn together in the common responsibility and joy of rearing children who are exclusively dependent upon them. Moreover, women have a special stake in the family because their status is ordinarily derived from the jobs of their husbands rather than from their own occupational achievements.

The family obligation in American society is well buttressed, but it shows signs of weakening. The incentives employed to support the family obligation might well be directed elsewhere. That is, Americans might conceivably fulfill their sexual drives, overcome their loneliness, and rear their children largely outside the nuclear family. In an era of increasing sexual freedom, and at a time when preschooling is becoming more and more popular, there are trends in this direction. Women already have considerable freedom to gain their own status in the occupational world. To be sure, the very suggestion that the family might not be essential is probably rather shocking to most Americans. And the fact that the suggestion is shocking indicates that the family obligation remains rather solidly entrenched. It is far too much a part of the world that we take for granted to be readily set aside.

Indeed, both the job and the family obligations are so completely taken for granted that it may well seem to the reader quite unnecessary for me to have described in such detail these obvious facts. But what is not so obvious is the power our society possesses through these culturally prescribed obligations to control our lives. This is what I wish to stress. The very fact that faithful performance in the job and in the family is so completely accepted as obligatory reveals the power our society wields to ensure our support for the existing order. Our society successfully wields this power only partly because it exercises powerful sanctions, such as giving or withholding income and status in order to ensure performance in the job. It is successful also because it has induced us to accept these obligations as obvious, normal, and natural.

Impact of the Job and Family Obligations Upon Social Action

The family in the United States, as evidence regarding its relationships to other features of the social system clearly indicates, is subordinate to occupation. What effect does this have upon social action?

One of the two channels for the expression of social action in American society is the job; the other is the voluntary association. The family, with rare exceptions, lacks power to serve as a channel for social action. Although individual members of the family can participate in economic and political activities, they seldom do so as family members. They simply do so "as individuals."[26] The family has great power in shaping the personalities of individuals and in influencing their morale. But it could hardly be said to possess independent power. In the total social system, the family is far more shaped by other institutions than it shapes them. The American kinship system, with its dominant pattern of the nuclear family, has developed as an accommodation to the needs of the occupational system, which in turn is essential for the functioning of the existing economic and political orders. Thus the family shapes personalities that can function well in supporting the existing social order. To be sure, parents who are concerned about social action can do much to instill a like concern in their children.[27] But such a concern does not readily emerge or flourish in a society that erects formidable obstacles against motivation for social action.

It is incumbent upon us in American society to work in the

very jobs that might become channels for social action. But our occupational system rarely offers jobs in any activities that fail to support the existing order. If the instruments of social control enforcing the job obligation were no more powerful than those enforcing the family obligation, Americans would have more freedom for social action through the job. Unfortunately, it is the job and not the family that is a channel for social action. The more powerful instruments of social control are focused on the job obligation. The inducements and the pressures that our social system exerts through these instruments of social control to ensure the sort of faithful job performance that provides powerful support for the existing order and that militates against social action will be analyzed in detail in Chapters 7 and 8. As for the voluntary association, the chances for social action through this channel will be discussed in Chapters 5 and 6.

The day-to-day functioning of our society depends heavily upon its success in gaining acceptance of the obligations to perform faithfully at the job and in the family. Both these obligations, which are inseparably tied together in our social system, direct our activity toward maintaining the existing order and, for the most part, away from social action. Thus, while ensuring that urgent, immediate needs will be met, our society ensures that urgent, long-range needs will not be met.

4

A Close Look
at Social Action

THE MAIN BUSINESS of these pages remains to be done. This is
the task of dealing with evidence that supports our fundamental thesis—namely, that in American society far too little
impulse toward social action exists, because, according to the
values of American culture and within the structure of the
American social system, social action is merely voluntary. But
before we get on with this main business, some clarification of
what is meant by "social action" is in order.

The Goal of Social Action

I have stated that social action is work to bring about change
in the institutions of society in the direction of justice and reconciliation. Part of the problem that we encounter in defining
social action comes from the difficulty involved in giving any
fixed definition of justice that can be applied meaningfully in
concrete situations. This is a complicated problem upon which
many volumes have been written,[1] and with which I cannot
hope to deal within the scope of this present book. In any case,
a decision about the nature of justice must be made anew in
each new problem situation. I assume that enough consensus
about the nature of justice exists among those concerned about
social action so that, in a specific problem situation, such people can keep their lines of communication open while they

struggle toward an agreement on how to express their concern together in action. I shall mention here only a rule of thumb to indicate what I consider to be the goal of social action.

I would say that it is the goal of social action to move in the *direction* of justice. To put it negatively, social action must move *away* from injustice, which, as Bruce Morgan points out, is much easier to discern than is justice.[2] Moving in the direction of justice requires that efforts be made to redress imbalances of power and privilege in favor of the relatively powerless and underprivileged so that the opportunities and the goods that are available in the society may be shared as widely as possible. Moving in the direction of justice also requires that the resources and the energies of the society be directed if necessary away from the vulgar and the trivial toward that which truly enriches, humanizes, and relieves distress. Thus, moving toward justice requires that special attention be given to the needs and rights of the disadvantaged, and to the public as a whole. Reconciliation, as Paul Lehmann points out, can be reached in society only as we pass through justice.[3]

Social Action Is Not Social Welfare

Sometimes it is difficult to distinguish what is and what is not social action. Especially problematic are activities that contribute to health, education, and welfare. These activities, which include the broad range of tasks involved in social work, are generally intended to benefit the disadvantaged and the whole community—precisely the groups to which social action directs its attention. The question arises whether any activity and especially any improvement in these areas is to be identified as social action. No answer, sufficiently definitive to separate clearly all instances of social action from all that are not, can be given. Again I shall suggest only a rule of thumb.

I would say that any activity or improvement in the services our society offers in health, education, or welfare, or in similar areas of endeavor, is *not* social action if it expresses or grows out of some already existing commitment of the community or of a part of the community. Such commitments, if they are indeed established commitments, are part of the existing order. Much valuable and needed activity can be carried on within the existing order, and innovations and improvements can even be introduced without the necessity for any changes in that fundamental element of the existing order, its existing commitments. Indeed, many needed innovations and improvements can be expressions of the society's existing commitments. Therefore, much of the needed change that is brought about in society is not social action.

Some illustrations may help. The erection of a new school, for example, is ordinarily an expression of an existing commitment. Certainly when a new suburban community is built, it can be expected that its middle-class inhabitants will be committed to the education of their children and that they will build a new school if this is necessary for their children to be educated. A good deal of initiative and voluntary effort may be needed to get the school built, but since this activity would grow out of an already existing commitment, it would not, according to my rule of thumb, qualify as social action. On the other hand, few cities are committed to providing first-class educational facilities to disadvantaged people living in slum areas. They are committed to providing schools, to be sure—all too often ill-equipped, overcrowded, and with underpaid teachers. The talent and expense devoted to schools in deprived areas must be much greater than that devoted to schools in privileged areas if there is to be more nearly equal opportunity in education. Rather vigorous social action might well be required to bring about the erection and staffing of more adequate schools in inner-city neighborhoods. The initial achievement of this goal, however, might not guarantee continued community support. Continued social action might be necessary to ensure a continuingly adequate teaching staff for such a school if the community was not solidly committed to paying for better teachers and a low student-teacher ratio. Thus, initiating needed health, education, and welfare services for groups in the society which have not had access to them would qualify as social action. But it appears to me that improving such services for privileged groups that have come to expect them is not a matter of social action.

Social work, which is especially directed toward helping disadvantaged people, may be confused with social action. But social work has traditionally helped individuals and families without making effort to change the structure of the society which renders them disadvantaged. Indeed, social work has served very effectively in supporting the existing order. It has helped marginal individuals to function better in the society without challenging the existing status system or the existing structures of power. It may help an individual to gain sufficient self-confidence so that he can initiate social action, but this has ordinarily been only an indirect consequence of social work. I get the impression that professional social workers are now coming increasingly to see a need for social action. But it appears to me that a distinction between social work and social action is still useful and legitimate.

Another example: The ongoing program of the National Foundation for Infantile Paralysis and its March of Dimes is not, according to my rule of thumb, social action, because the Foundation has had since 1933 a broad base of solid public support.[4] The founding of this association, however, probably qualifies as social action. Although most social action is probably controversial, this example indicates that it need not be, because the Foundation drew immediate support from the public.

Still another example: The fact that the Southern Christian Leadership Conference has a rather large, full-time, paid staff indicates that maintaining SCLC has become a rather well-established commitment in American society. To be sure, support for SCLC is by no means unanimous and is borne by only a small minority of Americans. Thus, an "existing commitment" of a community can result from active support by a small mi-nority. Although *support* of SCLC's full-time staff is probably no longer a matter of social action, the *activities* of the staff—directed toward changing the existing commitments of numer-ous communities across the United States—do qualify as social action. The fact that a well-established voluntary association can engage in social action provides an example of a rare phe-nomenon in our society: an institutionalized impulse toward social action.

The term "existing commitment" is another way of saying that something is "institutionalized." That which is institution-alized need not necessarily have some activity or organization to give it expression. It may simply be, at least temporarily, a firmly held value within a community. But such values are not likely to be discernible unless they are embodied in some activ-ity or organization. And even where commitments are thus em-bodied, it is not always clear how firm these commitments are. Thus, numerous difficulties can arise in the effort to determine what is and what is not social action. Nevertheless, seeing so-cial action as effort to bring about change in the existing com-mitments of a society (or part of a society) in the direction of justice and reconciliation provides a serviceable rule of thumb for identifying social action.

The Thrust of Social Action

Social action must not be confused with indiscriminate es-pousal of every "liberal" cause that happens along, or with un-critical support of the claims of every disadvantaged or dissi-dent group. We can well be profoundly grateful for the remarkable order that exists in American society. In the United States we enjoy a viable order with a considerable degree of justice and harmony. We have means for redressing injustices in orderly and peaceful ways. Such a remarkable order is not easily come by in this troubled world. The contrasting histories

of many other peoples point up the difficulty and the value of
the American achievement of order. In many societies social
change has been accompanied by far more violence than in
ours. Those concerned with social action in the United States
must be sensitive to the need for preserving the American
achievement of order. We must become aware of elements in
our society which can disrupt order—of existing and potential
injustice and alienation among men which can break into open,
destructive conflict. We must attempt to initiate change before
disruptive injustice and alienation can do irreparable damage
to our society. In order to carry out this function, we must
avoid becoming unduly committed to the *existing* order. We
must not go about "saying, 'Peace, peace,' when there is no
peace" (Jer. 8:11). Rather, we must be constantly working to
change the existing order to make possible a more viable, a
more harmonious, a more just, and a more stable social order.

It is a blessing of incalculable value that the American political system provides instruments through which change can
come about in an orderly manner. But change does not come
about as easily as American democratic ideology, expressed,
for example, in the incredible naïveté of American high school
civics textbooks, would lead one to believe. There are in American society informal arrangements of power, and there are
well-established habits, traditions, and customs that are not
mentioned in civics textbooks, and that are highly resistant to
change. These elements of resistance to change help provide
stability, an indispensable need in society. But they can also
aggravate and perpetuate sources of injustice among men. In-
sofar as they do, the stability they contribute is reduced, even
while the illusion of stability may continue. Those taking responsibility for social action must be willing to make extraordinary efforts—efforts well beyond their routine obligations as
defined by the existing order—to overcome these resistances to
change, these resistances to a truly stable order, by working
assiduously to overcome existing and potential sources of alienation and injustice in the society.

Now, to be sure, certain types of change are a normal part of the existing order in American society. Constant innovation in industry, both in technology and in organization,[5] rising national product, increasing productivity, expansion of various forms of Social Security, all in the midst of a rapidly growing population—these changes, while for the most part consciously sought, are largely unconsciously assumed to be a desirable part of the existing order. That is, Americans tend to take for granted the desirability of these changes without really evaluating their consequences. The changes that are sought frequently produce disruption in other sectors of the society where change is resisted. For example, automation in industry places a high premium on technical and managerial talent, and thus there is a diminishing demand for unskilled labor. A large unemployment problem has resulted, especially affecting the unskilled, educated population of our central cities. As successful managers and technicians move to the suburbs, the money and talent that might help remedy the inner cities' problems are drained away. Accordingly, poor educational facilities are provided for the very people who most desperately need education. Thus the American social system tends to work to its own detriment. It lacks sufficient built-in sources of initiative to cope with such problems. It is a society against itself.

The Demanding Nature of Social Action

Initiative in social action, despite its suffering the disadvantage of being merely voluntary according to the values of American culture, is desperately needed. But those who wish to respond to this desperate need must make no mistake about the demanding nature of the task that needs to be performed.

Few activities in our society, even among our socially prescribed obligations, are more demanding than is the task of initiating social action. It requires exceptional initiative, energy, and persistence, because established customs and interests are extremely difficult to dislodge. It requires tact and sensitivity, because one who engages in social action is trying to bring about justice and reconciliation among human beings—including himself—who find it very difficult to see that their own interests can be a source of injustice. It requires intelligence in order that social issues, whose ramifications can be overwhelmingly complex, may be clearly understood. It requires a willingness to work without immediate achievement of goals, and without promise of favorable recognition. And, indeed, it requires a willingness to risk opposition and disapproval.

Engaging in social action—and especially initiating social action—demands about as much talent, skill, and drive as the sort of work that is done in professional and in managerial positions in our society. It would be useful for the man who engages in social action to have at least a college education—partly for the intellectual development and partly for the self-confidence that can be gained thereby. He may be frequently dealing, for example, with issues whose legal ramifications alone call for considerable educational background and intellectual sophistication. In his dealing with people who occupy positions of power in the community, it is helpful if his education and intelligence can match theirs. But unfortunately, the most talented, educated people are generally drawn off into professional and managerial positions that commit them to spend their time and energies in supporting various aspects of the existing order. Professional and managerial positions at the higher levels are rightly filled with people who have gained considerable experience in their work under the guidance of more experienced personnel. By the same token, competent leadership in social action requires considerable experience. However, the opportunities to gain experience in social action under the tutelage of skilled, experienced practitioners are extremely rare. An individual can, of course, attempt to plunge into social action without experience—and in many situations this is the only way to get started. But discouragement may come quickly to one lacking experience because one is likely to make mistakes or run up against obstacles that appear insurmountable. Most of those who would engage in social action suffer the disadvantage of being rank amateurs in areas—notably the political and economic orders—dominated by professionals.

Despite its very demanding nature, however, great numbers of people in our society, trained for responsible roles in our occupational system, have the ability to initiate social action. Moreover, I would stick by my earlier contention that few people lack the abilities needed to make important contributions in social action.[6] If they do not have the abilities for initiating it, then most people at least have the abilities for assisting and supporting those who take leadership roles.

Although the task of initiating most types of social action is fully as demanding as work in professional and in managerial positions, yet our social system offers for social action very little of the obvious immediate reward in status, or of the concrete, tangible reward in income, that it provides as incentives to ensure the fulfillment of burdensome job obligations. A man may perhaps harbor some precarious hope of gaining status or at least recognition through social action, but he can hardly expect to gain income from it.[7] In short, our social system, which greatly needs an impulse toward the difficult work of social action, fails to provide anywhere near the propulsive force in that direction that it provides to secure fulfillment of job obligations.

Beginning in Social Action

Although American society raises great obstacles against initiative in social action, it does not forbid such activity, and places few limitations upon those who are willing to make the required effort. One of the most difficult steps in making this effort, especially for those who have had no previous experience in it, is simply getting started. How does one begin? By way of answer, I shall present only a few rather obvious observations.

Already I have mentioned the necessity for choosing some single, limited social problem, for finding a few other people who share the same concern, and for deciding together to work persistently at this problem over a long period of time, recognizing that a great deal of work is necessary to achieve a small social change.[8] But how does one deal with the prior matter of choosing the problem?

Obviously a person ought to focus his attention on some social problem that he can realistically visualize as being within the scope of his influence, a problem that is in some way accessible. An individual who does not already possess some special power in the economic or political order probably ought to focus on some problem in his own local community. Or, recognizing that the urgent problems of the inner city are inseparable from the existence of suburbia, even though suburban dwellers usually disclaim responsibility for them, he might focus, if he lives in a suburban community, on some problem in the nearby urban center, where he is perhaps employed. After working for a time on a problem at the local level, a person may find it necessary, in order to accomplish what needs to be done, to deal with officials of the state and national governments. But he need not begin working at this level and need not be intimidated by the prospect. When the necessity becomes apparent, he and his fellow workers can learn how to exert influence at these more distant levels of power. Of course, a person's initial choice of a problem need not be limited to his local community. He might begin a group to focus attention on some aspect of our nation's foreign policy, might become informed in depth about the matter, and might try to gain support both from the public and from decision-making public officials for some change in policy. But wherever an individual begins, he ought to be reasonably confident that the problem is accessible to his understanding and influence.

A second criterion for choice of an issue is, of course, its urgency and importance. The more a social problem threatens justice and order in society, the more urgent it is. The more intensive and extensive its impact, the more important it is. The American social order is so intimately bound up with the whole world order that few, if any, social problems at the local level lack international implications. I would suggest that the choice of issues upon which to act be based partly, therefore, upon what is most urgent in the light of the total world situation. An obviously urgent and important issue today in the light of the total world situation is the problem of racism— a problem very close at hand for most Americans.

A third matter involved in choice of an issue is the channel through which one attempts to carry on social action. A person must decide whether he can make a more effective contribution through his job or through some voluntary association. For many this decision is quite simple. Social action through the job is not feasible for many people since they possess so little power in their jobs, either because they work at the lower levels of great bureaucratic organizations where they have little influence over policy or because they work with small enterprises that themselves have little power. Those who do exercise considerable power in their jobs, however, ought to think seriously whether they might use their power for social action. Whatever an individual may decide about his job, the voluntary association remains an open possibility. Existing voluntary associations involved in social action are ordinarily delighted to have the services of dedicated new members. But if existing associations are failing to meet or even to face existing problems, a person remains free to start his own voluntary association. This option has some great advantages which I shall mention toward the end of Chapter 9.

It is perhaps possible that an original, informal, initiating group of concerned people may be able to carry on a program of social action directly, without developing the paraphernalia of a typical voluntary association. But it may be forced to call for the support of other people, perhaps many other people, in order to command greater power. With a large membership, a formal structure usually becomes necessary. The initiating group may have to move toward developing a formal organization with a constitution, bylaws, elected officers, regular dues, and the like. In its early days the association may well arouse a good deal of enthusiasm, but as it grows, the members' sense of participation and influence in an exciting, significant new movement is likely to diminish. Then the association's commitment to social action must be energetically maintained by the initiating group and by any others it can co-opt.

Whether social action be expressed through the voluntary association or through the job, it usually needs the impetus and the sustenance that can be provided only by some small, dedicated, informal, initiating group. Such a group is quite different in size and in structure from the formal voluntary association. Nevertheless, among the great variety of voluntary activities that are carried on in American society, social action has much in common with active participation in voluntary associations. Therefore, an analysis of patterns of participation in voluntary associations and of the reasons for these patterns, as provided in the next two chapters, can do much to indicate why there is so little impulse toward social action in American society.

5

Weakness of the Impulse Toward Social Action as Revealed in an Analysis of Voluntary Associations

SOCIAL ACTION, effort to bring about social change in the direction of justice and reconciliation, requires that the existing social order be challenged and modified. The American social system allows freedom for the expression of social action, and American ideology even specifies it as a responsibility of citizenship. In practice, however, it meets stiff resistance because the actual realities of daily existence in American society strongly discourage involvement in social action. Although it is not forbidden, its importance is effectively denied since American culture, in deed if not in word, defines it as merely voluntary. Meanwhile, our social system exercises powerful instruments of social control to guarantee faithful performance of job and family obligations which overwhelmingly support the existing order. Hence it is very difficult for Americans to initiate or to sustain social action, despite the fact that it is greatly needed for the health of the very society that resists it.

Since social action is voluntary, it must be carried on during leisure time. Fulfilling obligations, especially to the job and to the family, consumes a very great proportion of the individual's waking hours and leaves him rather little leisure time.[1] But the amount of leisure time available in our society has been increasing.[2] If they wished, therefore, Americans could be spending an increasing proportion of their leisure time in social action. I do not know of any empirical study that could throw light on this matter, but I suspect that the time spent in social action has not increased in proportion with the growth in leisure time. I suspect that the impulse toward social action in American society is dependent not so much upon an increase in free time as it is dependent upon more effective incentives. People manage to make time for matters that they consider important.

The Uses of Leisure Time

The fact of the matter is that the great bulk of leisure time in America is consumed in activities that require little effort or discipline and that offer immediate satisfaction or gratification. There has been little systematic study of this matter. But a careful piece of research done in Westchester County over three decades ago on the leisure and nonleisure activities of men and women of all classes indicated that nearly 90 percent of the average adult's leisure time was devoted to eating, visiting, reading (other than study or work), entertainment, sports, listening to the radio, and motoring.[3] Less than 3 percent of leisure time was spent in "club activities," although for a minority of the people it was much higher. The remaining 10 percent or so of leisure time was spent in "miscellaneous" activities including church attendance and activities, active participation in the arts, nonbusiness correspondence and telephoning, idling, and others not readily classified.[4]

If the results of this study can be taken as reasonably representative of the behavior of Americans in our own day, it is apparent that the great bulk of American leisure time is spent in activities that require nowhere near the self-discipline, persistence, effort, and willingness to postpone satisfactions that social action requires. Probably a good many people, if they had the will to do so, could make available much of this leisure time, which is now devoted to immediately gratifying pursuits and to relaxation, for social action. To be sure, many could claim with justification that during a good bit of their leisure time they are engaging in activities with their families, and thus are fulfilling one of their fundamental obligations. The above study does not take this possibility into account. Nevertheless, it appears that, in general, people do not need more time as much as they need more incentive to engage in social action. Incentive is not easily come by for the very demanding and often controversial task of social action which must be carried on during people's "free time" when they feel that they have a right to rest and to recreation.

Participation in Voluntary Associations and Motivation for Social Action

More complete data on the use of leisure time in America could go a long way toward indicating the degree to which Americans are willing to commit their time and energies to social action. Another way in which the extent of this commitment can be seen in greater detail is through an analysis of participation in voluntary associations. Although there is little data available which measures directly the extent of participation in social action, there have been a good many studies of participation in voluntary associations. Social action is probably closer akin to participation in voluntary associations than it is to any other type of leisure-time activity.

To be precise, I should say that engaging in social action—and especially initiating social action—is distantly akin to *membership* in voluntary associations, but is closely akin to *active participation* in voluntary associations. It is most closely akin to the most active sort of participation, namely, to *leadership* in voluntary associations. Indeed, engaging in social action can be classified for purposes of analysis as a type of voluntary association leadership. Such leadership requires the special managerial ability and inclination which I have mentioned as necessary for social action. Except possibly for the cases of a few professional executives of associations, it is voluntary activity calling for the donation of a great deal of leisure time and requiring a high degree of personal commitment. We can expect that an analysis of the patterns of leadership in voluntary associations can throw a great deal of light on the possibilities for social action. Before the phenomenon of leadership in associations can be adequately gauged and understood, however, some knowledge of the number and variety of voluntary associations in the United States and some analysis of the extent of their membership are necessary.

Prominence of Voluntary Associations in America

The voluntary association, which is characteristic of American society and has proliferated here more than in most other countries, is part of the cultural milieu that we take for granted and assume to be a normal and natural element in our social order. It is the institution through which we virtually instinctively pursue interests outside the bounds of the job and the family which require cooperation with others.

Many observers have commented upon the extraordinary number and variety of voluntary associations in the United States. As long ago as the 1830's, Alexis de Tocqueville reported:

> In no country in the world has the principle of association been more successfully used, or more unsparingly applied to a multitude of different objects, than in America.[5]

There is evidence that, since the famous French traveler wrote these words, voluntary associations may have proliferated more rapidly than the U.S. population. At least the Lynds in their study of Middletown, observed that between 1890 and 1924 voluntary associations had proliferated about 50 percent more rapidly than the town's population.[6]

Every local community has an abundance of associations. A

study of 140 rural villages in 1930 revealed that they had among them 2,909 local voluntary associations—about one association for each 165 persons.[7] In 1924, Middletown had 458 "active clubs" for its population of 38,000—approximately one for each eighty people.[8] Warner and Lunt found an even greater density of associations in Yankee City during the early 1930's. With a population of about 17,000 there were 899 voluntary associations—roughly one for each nineteen persons.[9]

There are literally thousands of voluntary associations in the United States organized at the national level. The *Encyclopedia of Associations* in its fourth edition listed some 8,800,[10] and this was not an exhaustive list. While many of these organizations are quite small, some are enormous. The American Farm Bureau Federation, for example, claimed in 1964 to have 1,600,000 members in 50 state groups, with 2,700 county farm bureaus,[11] and the National Congress of Parents and Teachers reported 12,100,000 members, 52 state branches, 46,962 local groups, and 60 full-time staff members.[12] Sherwood Fox, whose dissertation lists, classifies, and analyzes more than 5,000 associations of national scope, comments that these associations "are only a very small fraction of the estimated quarter of a million associations at national, state, and local levels in the United States."[13]

A great many voluntary associations are sufficiently in the public eye that they gain a good deal of publicity. In almost any issue of almost any community's daily newspaper, one can find mention of activities of some voluntary association. Although many associations are so obscure that hardly anyone but their members is aware of their existence, others exercise a good deal of power and influence. Voluntary associations are sufficiently numerous, sufficiently publicized, and sufficiently powerful that they occupy a very prominent place in American society.

Extent of Membership in Voluntary Associations

Since voluntary associations are so numerous in the United States, and since some have such large memberships, one can easily get the impression that most Americans must belong to several associations. This is not the case, however. Numerous empirical studies conducted in various communities all over the United States have indicated consistently that a large proportion of Americans belong to no association—the proportion varying between 30 percent and 60 percent in various parts of the country.[14]

Secondary analysis of two national opinion surveys, which were not concerned directly with voluntary association membership, confirmed the findings of the community studies. Data gathered by the American Institute of Public Opinion in 1954 indicated that 45 percent of Americans belonged to no association. Data gathered by the National Opinion Research Center in 1955 showed that 64 percent belonged to no association. In neither study was church membership included. Probably an accurate figure would lie somewhere in between.[15]

Active Minority, Inactive Majority

In addition to the fact that large numbers of the American people belong to no association at all, among those who do belong only a minority participates actively. There are two ways by which active participation can be gauged. One is by the proportion of people who hold several memberships, and the other is by the proportion of people who are intensely active in any one association. The second is more useful for my purposes here, since I am interested in intense participation which is akin to social action. For some people, the holding of multiple memberships may indicate a distinct unwillingness to become deeply involved in any one association. Such a pattern of behavior is, of course, incompatible with social action. It would seem more likely, however, that a large proportion of the people who hold multiple memberships would be intensely active in at least one association, or are at least willing and able to become intensely active.

Available studies indicate that only a very few people hold several memberships each in voluntary associations. Goldhamer in his study of 5,500 residents of Chicago found that 20 percent of all the memberships were held by 4 percent of the people, who had five or more memberships each. These active joiners held as many memberships as the 60 percent least active of the population.[16] Bushee found in Boulder, Colorado, that 71 percent of the adult population held at least one membership (including church membership) in some voluntary association. Of these joiners, 54 percent belonged to only one, 23 percent to two, 11 percent to three, 5 percent to four, and 3 percent to five. Only 2.5 percent of the total population or 3.5 percent of those belonging to any voluntary association held memberships in more than five associations.[17] This study shows a remarkably steady drop in the proportion holding memberships as the number of memberships per person increases. Both studies, of course, indicate quite clearly that only a small proportion of the population, judging by the criterion of multiple memberships, is highly active in voluntary associations.

That many of the people who hold multiple memberships may also be intensely active in at least one association is indicated in Sills's study of the National Foundation for Infantile Paralysis. The Foundation, whose program was carried on by two separate types of local organizations—the local chapters which operated throughout the year and the March of Dimes organization which put on a yearly fund-raising campaign—managed to maintain a remarkably high degree of activity among its members. It did this by having as members only people who took on specific jobs. The March of Dimes organization was dispersed after its two-month campaign so that the unenthusiastic were weeded out yearly. Both the chapters and the March of Dimes organization were advised by the national headquarters to recruit as members only people who were already members of several other organizations. According to Sills's study, a majority of Foundation volunteers belonged to several associations. Only 4 percent of the chapter volunteers and only 2 percent of the March of Dimes volunteers belonged to no other organization.[18] Thus there seems to be at least some slight evidence that a sizable proportion of the people who hold multiple memberships can be expected to be intensely active in one or more associations. Indeed, judging by the Foundation's policy of recruiting busy people, it seems likely that it would be rather difficult to find outside the group that holds multiple memberships people who are willing to participate actively in associations. Of course, those who hold several memberships are only a small proportion of our total population.

In almost any particular voluntary association, the phenomenon of an active minority and of an inactive majority prevails. Intense activity in associations is left to a very few.

> No matter what interest any particular association represents, we find the existence of an active minority in control. In the "service clubs," for example, there is a very active nucleus and a large group who are "just members." Although each club has many committees and every member is expected to be active on at least one of them, many members are wholly inactive.[19]

So well known and so widely deplored is this American pattern of the inactive majority that it hardly needs documentation. There have been, nevertheless, some empirical studies which provide concrete, statistical evidence for the pattern. Brunner and Kolb studied adult membership in voluntary associations in 140 rural villages located in all parts of the United States. In these villages there were 2,838 voluntary associations in 1924 and 2,909 associations in 1930, not counting churches and church-related activities. Brunner and Kolb found that the average percentage of the memberships which attended organization meetings was 35.6 percent in 1924 and 34.7 percent in 1930.[20] Bushee found a somewhat higher average attendance at organization meetings in Boulder, Colorado, which, as a university city, in about 1940 probably had a better educated population (although students were not included in the survey), more inclined to participate in associations. The average attendance at voluntary association meetings was 51.4 percent.[21] These figures are enough to indicate that a large proportion of association members are inactive. But since the figures only reveal attendance at meetings, the bare minimum of participation, they do not give an accurate picture of the intensity of participation in associations.

Data from the Detroit Area Study collected in about 1952 indicated rather clearly that the great majority of voluntary association members are at best only slightly active in their associations. Sixty-three percent of the "probability sample" of 749 adults interviewed in the study belonged to some formal association (not including churches). These members were asked about their activities in voluntary associations during the three months preceding the interviews. Twenty-four percent had attended no association meetings during this time, 34 percent had attended only one or two meetings, 23 percent had attended at least three meetings, and 19 percent had attended at least three meetings and in addition either held some office or committee membership or had participated outside of regular meetings on at least two occasions.[22] Thus only about 19 percent of the people who belonged to associations, about 12 percent of the total population, could be said to be active in some association—and even in this study, the criteria for a high degree of activity are not very rigorous. Of course, in any one average association, the active minority would probably be much smaller than 19 percent because many of these active people very likely held several memberships, but were listed as "very active" if they fulfilled the criteria for this category through any one association.

Job and Family Obligations
vs. Voluntary Participation

The data presented thus far do little more than confirm the already well-known fact that social action is rather rare in American society. Social action is, of course, only one activity among many others that are carried on in and by voluntary associations, and it is an exceptionally demanding activity at that. Therefore, it can be expected to comprise only a small proportion of the most active participation in voluntary associations. The limited extent of membership and the low level of active participation in voluntary associations in American society point toward the minute degree of commitment toward social action that is to be found, or is likely to be found.

But why should active participation be so limited and what light can this throw upon the scarcity of social action? The most obvious explanation for the inactivity of the majority and for the rarity of leadership initiative and talent in associations lies in a fundamental fact that has already been mentioned, namely, the priority that job and family obligations take over most individuals' time and energies. Barber puts the matter this way:

> Because of the individual's culturally prescribed preoccupation in the United States with obligations to his job and his "isolated conjugal family," there exists a socially structured pull away from membership in even those voluntary associations relevant to his interests. Further, even when he is a member of an association, the individual's interest is so limited that it leads to minimal participation.[23]

Job and family obligations are obstacles to motivation for social action largely because they consume a great deal of time, but not only for this reason. Despite the fact that they are time-consuming, there is quite a bit of leisure that is po-

tentially available for activity in associations. But these obligations are obstacles to social action also because people, through
fulfilling them, can gain confidence that they have carried out
adequately all that society requires of them. For very few people is there any social stigma in their failure to participate
actively in voluntary associations—especially if they perform
their job and family obligations notably well. Not only does
our culture *define* our primary responsibilities, but it also tends
to *confine* our interests to these limited areas. Thus Americans'
leisure-time interests drift toward immediately self-gratifying
pursuits. They fulfill their job and family responsibilities
largely because they are obligated to do so. They engage in
sports and seek entertainment largely because they enjoy
them. They avoid active participation in voluntary associations
largely because they do not enjoy it and because they are not
obligated to do so.

This is part of the picture. But, of course, this explanation
is rather too simple. The fact remains that some people do
participate actively in voluntary associations—at least, enough
do so to provide leadership for many thousands of associations
across the country. How can we account for their activity? Is it
to be explained purely in psychological terms as a matter of
personal inclination and personal preference? Psychological
factors are, of course, very much involved. But they are by no
means the only factors. Of crucial importance for participation
in voluntary associations is the rather elusive but nonetheless
conspicuous reality of social class. Both membership and
leadership in associations have, in numerous empirical studies,
been closely correlated with class.

Association Membership and Class

It has been found, with consistent results from all areas of
the United States, that a greater proportion of the higher
classes than of the lower classes belongs to voluntary associa-

tions. Warner and Lunt employed their own characteristic
system of class stratification in a study of membership in voluntary associations in Yankee City, and reported the following
results:

> Approximately 72% of the people in the upper classes
> belong to associations, 64% of the upper-middle class,
> and only 49% of the lower-middle class. The percentages
> continue to drop as one moves down the class levels, for
> only 39% of the upper-lower and 22% of the lower-lower
> class are members of associations.[24]

Not only does a greater proportion of the people of higher
classes hold membership in at least one association, but also
the higher the class, the greater the proportion of people who
hold more than one membership. Indeed, the class differences
are considerably more marked when the criterion of voluntary
participation is not just membership in one association or
more, but when the criterion is multiple memberships. For
example, Warner and Lunt found that among association members in the upper-upper class 49 percent belonged to three or
more associations, while in the lower-lower class 7 percent belonged to three or more. This proportion for the upper-uppers
is seven times as great as that for the lower-lowers, whereas
the proportion of upper-uppers belonging to only one association (or more) is only three and a half times as great as the
corresponding proportion of lower-lowers. The rates of membership in three or more associations for the other classes are:
lower-upper, 47 percent; upper-middle, 38 percent; lower-mid-
dle, 20 percent; upper-lower, 12 percent.[25]

Data from the national samples of the American Institute of
Public Opinion and the National Opinion Research Center
polls mentioned above indicate a consistent increase in the
percentage of people holding one association membership or
multiple memberships as their education increases, as their
income increases, and as higher occupational ratings are
reached.[26] Indeed, this relationship between social class and

membership in voluntary associations has been well documented by studies from all over the country. The higher the class—whether class be determined solely by education, or by occupation, or by income, or by more complicated criteria— the greater the proportion of people belonging to voluntary associations and the greater the proportion of people who hold memberships in more than one association. These "uniformities hold for all types of areas in the country."[27]

Association Leadership and Class

Given the facts (1) that a greater proportion of the higher classes than of the lower classes holds association memberships, and (2) that a still greater proportion of the higher classes holds multiple memberships, the implication that leadership in voluntary associations is concentrated among people of the higher classes appears unavoidable. In addition to these facts about membership, there are other indications that this is, indeed, the case. Since leadership is more difficult to pinpoint than is membership, however, the evidence supporting the contention that leadership in associations is concentrated among the higher classes is not as full as it is for the correlation between membership and class.

A study in Franklin, Indiana, in 1940 divided a sample of the adult population into approximately equal groups, an upper class with family earnings over $100 a month, and a lower class with family earnings under $100 a month.[28] Leadership in voluntary associations, "defined as the holding of an office, membership on boards of control, teaching of a Sunday school class, or acting as chairman of committees,"[29] was compared for each of the two classes. It was discovered that in the lower class each man held on the average only .08 leadership positions, and each woman only .11 leadership positions. In the upper class each man held an average of .35, and each woman .28 leadership positions. Education was also considered as a factor affecting leadership. In the upper class, 86 college men averaged .61 leaderships, 74 high school men .31 leaderships, and 27 grade school men .11 leaderships.[30]

Another research project, carried out in Evanston, Illinois, divided a sample of the white, male, native-born, adult population equally into a higher and a lower class according to three criteria: occupation, income, and education. With leadership being defined as holding or having held an office in an association, it was found that the higher class provided a significantly, although not spectacularly, higher proportion of the leadership in voluntary associations. With the classes divided according to occupation, the higher class provided 58 percent more; according to income, 103 percent more; and according to education, 69 percent more of the leadership than the lower class provided.[31]

While the concrete, statistical evidence for the preponderance of the higher classes in the leadership of voluntary associations is not voluminous, it at least is unambiguous, and confirms the conclusions of many observers. Among these observers are Warner and Lunt, who comment that the two upper classes

> are more active in the associational structure within the limits of their size than are any others. The smallness of their numbers permit persons of the upper classes to make an effort as a group to exert control over the society through this medium. Although the members of these two classes often do not hold offices in the controlling hierarchies of the various groups, they nevertheless effectively exercise certain pressures upon those who do.[32]

Warner and Lunt do not attempt to give evidence for their view. This may be partly because leadership in associations is often very difficult to identify and to trace with accuracy, and partly because such concentration of leadership is widely believed to exist within practically every community.

In their statement, Warner and Lunt indicate another dimension of the problem of association leadership. They intimate that certain people of the higher classes, who have a good deal of influence and power in the community, exercise in the associations what might better be called "control" than "leadership," not because the two terms are mutually exclusive, but because "control" points more clearly to what actually happens.

Reasons for Concentration of Association Leadership Among People of the Higher Classes

Why should leadership in voluntary associations be heavily concentrated among people of the higher social classes? What effect does this concentration of leadership have upon the impulse toward social action in American society?

Gunnar Myrdal, the Swedish social scientist who has astutely analyzed American culture, sees the pattern of "individual leadership and mass passivity," with leadership coming predominantly from the higher classes, as a peculiarly American phenomenon deeply ingrained in our culture.[33] This pattern has developed despite an explicit "Jeffersonian" ideology of full participation. Myrdal expresses amazement that this pattern has been taken for granted not only by ordinary citizens but by social scientists as well.[34] He suggests that a major reason for this pattern is the higher degree of social mobility in the United States, which "drained the masses in every generation of most of their organizational catalysts."[35]

Leadership talent generally includes precisely the intelligence and the determination necessary for lower-class persons to gain higher education. This often enables them to move into occupational positions in business or the professions, thus giving them an identity no longer with the lower classes. The very structure of American society does not allow leadership ability to remain identified for very long with the lower classes. Rather, it entices people with such ability into occupations that change their class identity and interests. Conceivably, people with a former lower-class background might be candidates for social action, since they might be expected to understand some of the injustices suffered by the disadvantaged. But all too often they are eager to erase any vestige of their lower-class background in order to confirm their advance in status.

Even if people of ability rising out of the lower classes could be counted upon as a reservoir of leadership for social action, they would not provide a very large source of supply. A deep sense of discouragement pervades the lower classes so that they generally fail even to take advantage of many opportunities that are readily available to them. Serious economic and educational handicaps tend to reinforce each other —money is needed for gaining education, and education is needed for earning money. These handicaps tend to produce a lack of self-confidence and a sense of pessimism out of proportion to an objective analysis of the situation. Lower-class people tend to withdraw from activities that could contribute to their growth. They cut themselves off from experiences and from sources of information that could help develop their reasoning ability, their judgment, and their sense of confidence in relation to others. Hence the rarity of leadership from the lower classes.[36]

Conversely, the higher classes generally come easily into the qualifications necessary for association leadership. Not only are money and education readily available to them, but also they grow up from childhood with command of language and reasoning skill, with broad interests in the world around them, and with an incalculably valuable sense of self-confidence. Leadership positions are readily attained partly because of their ability, but also because other people automatically grant them deference. They may not even have to exert much effort or initiative in order to gain positions of leadership.

Implications for Social Action

The fact that in voluntary associations leadership is concentrated among people of the higher classes augurs ill for an impulse toward social action in American society. Since higher-class people occupy positions of privilege, their interests, as far as they are likely to see, lie in providing support for the existing order. Thus we have in our society a situation where those who have the ability and the training to provide initiative for social action are generally not interested in doing so. Their occupational and class interests tend to desensitize them to the urgent need for social action. On the other hand, lower-class people, whose immediate self-interest might well make them aware of needs for social action, seldom have training to equip them for it. Many of them may have sufficient ability, but they are likely to be too preoccupied with survival, too accustomed to submission, and, in short, too discouraged to have any real hope for social change.

Our hope for initiative in social action, short of outbursts of revolutionary violence from frustrated, disadvantaged, lower-class people, must rest largely upon people of the higher classes who are sensitive to existing alienation and injustice among men. I am sure there are many such people in the United States. There are people who recognize that their real, long-range self-interest lies in the elimination of injustice, however this may affect their own immediate interests. But can such people sustain initiative for the extraordinarily difficult tasks of social action when such work is merely voluntary in our society, and when their obligatory occupational and family involvements not only preempt their time and energies but also largely define their class identity and shape their outlook and interests so that they unconsciously spend the major portion of their time and energies in maintaining the existing order?

In American culture, the impulse toward social action is

pitifully weak. Those who are best equipped to carry on social action generally do not wish to do so. This is not due simply to the competition of job and family obligations for their time and talents, but also very largely it is due to the utter lack of any comparable sense of obligation to engage in social action. Fulfilling our culturally defined obligations to job and family does not necessarily lead us directly against social action. But it leads us in a different direction. It directs us toward preserving indiscriminately the existing order—much of which ought to be preserved, but much of which needs to be changed.

The present chapter, by describing patterns of participation in voluntary associations, and by explaining these patterns in the light of values that prevail in our society, has indirectly indicated how social pressures work against motivation for needed social action. The next chapter deals with the influence that existing voluntary associations themselves exert directly upon motivation for social action.

6

Existing Voluntary Associations

THE VOLUNTARY ASSOCIATION, one of the two channels available in American society for the expression of social action, is a prominent, although subordinate, element in our social system. As a subordinate element, it is more shaped by other elements—notably the political and economic orders—than it shapes them. Nevertheless, a large proportion of voluntary associations have at least the potentiality of serving as means for initiating social change. Representing groups of people, some of them quite large, they frequently exert influence amid the political and economic power structures of American society that cannot be ignored in the centers of power. To what extent do existing voluntary associations exert influence for change in behalf of social action—for change in the direction of justice and reconciliation?

This question is difficult to answer because the issue has a certain elusive quality. Quite different answers can appear plausible. For example, Arnold M. Rose and C. Wright Mills, looking at voluntary associations from quite different points of view, come to sharply differing conclusions regarding the possibilities for individuals to bring about social change (not necessarily social action as defined here) through them.

Clarifying an Elusive Issue

Rose is struck by the abundance of opportunities that voluntary associations offer the individual to participate in bringing about social change. He suggests that associations serve three important functions in facilitating the workings of democracy in the United States:

> (1) They *distribute power over social life* among a very large proportion of the citizenry, instead of allowing it to be concentrated in the elected representatives alone. . . . (2) The voluntary associations *provide a sense of satisfaction with modern democratic processes* because they help the ordinary citizen to see how the processes function in limited circumstances, of direct interest to himself, rather than as they grind away in a distant, impersonal, and incomprehensible fashion. (3) The voluntary associations *provide a social mechanism for continually instituting social changes,* so that the United States is a society in flux, constantly seeking . . . to solve long-standing problems and to satisfy new needs of groups of citizens as these needs arise.[1]

Rose recognizes the fact that voluntary associations are imperfect instruments for carrying out all these functions, especially since the lower classes participate in them very little. Including this major qualification, such claims as he makes for voluntary associations would seem to be quite indisputable. They seem simply to state the obvious. But they have an optimistic ring that is not always echoed elsewhere. Mills takes the pessimistic view in the following statement:

> Voluntary associations have become larger to the extent that they have become effective; and to just that extent they have become inaccessible to the individual who would shape by discussion the policies of the organization to which he belongs. Accordingly, along with older

institutions, these voluntary associations have lost their
grip on the individual. As more people are drawn into the
political arena, these associations become mass in scale;
and as the power of the individual becomes more dependent upon such mass associations, they are less accessible to the individual's influence.[2]

Although both writers acknowledge the power of associations,
their views concerning the individual's influence within them
differ rather sharply.

These views have obvious implications for social action.
Rose's view implies that abundant opportunities for social action are available in voluntary associations, whereas Mills's
position implies that existing voluntary associations profoundly
discourage people from initiating social action. Although these
two views appear to be in irreconcilable disagreement on the
facts, they really differ only in emphasis and in their subjective
response to the facts.

Rose finds cause for guarded optimism in the fact that
American society allows freedom for social action, and in the
fact that the voluntary association is a channel through which
anyone who wishes can take initiative for social change. As he
puts it:

> Any person who wishes . . . can usually join the leader-
> ship of most voluntary associations, if he is willing to
> spend the time and assume the responsibilities. . . .
>
> Through the voluntary association the ordinary citizen
> can acquire as much power in the community or the na-
> tion as his free time, ability, and inclinations permit him
> to, without actually going into the government service,
> provided he accepts the competition for power of other
> like-minded citizens.[3]

The position represented by Rose takes issue with Mills at an
important point. It may well be, as Mills says, that the large
association is likely to be "inaccessible to the individual who
would shape by discussion the policies of the organization."[4]

It is not clear, however, what Mills means by "discussion." How much effort and persistence does this involve? Mills seems to be deploring the fact that a little effort cannot accomplish great things. The fact of the matter, as I see it, is that a great deal of effort can often accomplish significant things if not great things.

But this is all very well where the initiative and drive for participation in voluntary associations already exists. Mills is quite properly concerned about the fact that modern voluntary associations have become so large that they discourage participation. Optimism like that of Rose is legitimate when we observe that there are plenty of opportunities to initiate social action through existing voluntary associations—at least, potential opportunities for highly motivated people. The opportunities are few in relation to the total number of associations, but offer abundant options to those who are willing to take initiative, and who have sufficient courage and imagination to see openings for social action where they are not apparent. But motivation for social action exists at present in all too meager measure. Pessimism like that of Mills is legitimate since we cannot expect existing voluntary associations to be very effective in arousing needed motivation for social action. Why they do so little to stimulate the needed motivation is our main interest in this chapter.

There are two kinds of facts about existing voluntary associations in the United States that especially affect motivation for social action. These are (1) the structure of voluntary associations and (2) the specific commitments and goals of voluntary associations.

The Structure of Large-Scale Voluntary Associations

I have already dealt with the phenomenon of the inactive majority and the active minority in associations. This phenomenon is due primarily to factors external to the associations: the priority of job and family obligations, the extremely demanding nature of leadership in associations, and the greater ability and self-confidence of people in the higher classes who play the more active role in associations. But it is also due to the requirements of organization within large associations themselves.

Most voluntary associations in the United States, however large they may be, establish a democratic organizational structure in order that there may be maximum participation by the membership. The attempt to establish democracy may not always be sincere. Even where it is not, however, the trappings of democracy must be displayed, because the practice has become thoroughly established in our culture. Where the trappings are present there is always some possibility for actual democracy.

But the low level of active participation in voluntary associations prevails despite widespread sincere efforts to encourage participation as much as possible by constituting associations along democratic lines. "In practically all voluntary associations, formal authority resides in the total membership."[5] To be sure, the *interests* of an association may be narrowly particularistic, and, in a sense, highly "undemocratic." Membership requirements, for example, may be narrowly exclusive. But it is the rare voluntary association whose internal structure is not explicitly democratic. The members vote for their officers in frequent elections, and official positions are frequently rotated. In business sessions, members vote on policy decisions, and in large associations which hold national conventions, the membership votes for delegates who in turn vote on policy matters. Where there are hired executives, democratic associations require regular and complete reports on their activities and especially on their expenditures, and the membership has the right to question their actions and to communicate their objections in meetings and in official publications.[6]

Nevertheless, most associations fail to achieve the demo-

cratic ideal of full member participation, and find their affairs
run by a small minority, as long as the majority feels that its
interests are being adequately served. The average union
member, for example, prefers not to bother with union meetings and is quite content to entrust his interests to the officials
if they succeed in exacting a steady flow of benefits from the
employer. Similarly, members of consumers' cooperative associations allow a minority to carry on their business and are
satisfied as long as they continue to reap some financial gain.[7]

The readiness of the majority to allow a few to carry out an
association's work is reinforced by organizational requirements
for the functioning of associations. Almost invariably someone
or some few people must carry out the "executive functions"
of the association.[8] These functions include coordinating the
energies of the organization within and acting in behalf of the
organization in relation to the world without. In a small, informal association, where communication among the members
is constant and a high degree of consensus exists, the executive
function may move informally from one member to another.
But the larger the organization, the greater the need for formal vesting of executive functions in one or in a few persons.
For the sake of consistency and efficiency in a large organization, one person or a small group needs the authority to carry
out the executive functions of the organization.

Carrying out executive functions often requires highly specialized knowledge about such matters as the purpose and history of the association and about precedents set by past actions. The demands of the executive role are often so great
that the members are all too willing to leave it to someone else,
and indeed, often it is necessary for large associations to hire
full-time executives. This leads to further centralization of
power. The hired executive with long tenure, although ranked
beneath the annually elected president, knows far more about
the association and is likely to exercise far more real power
than the elected officials whose jobs must rotate annually.
Since he is formally responsible to the members and subject

to dismissal by them, he may try to protect his job by keeping his movements as inconspicuous as possible and thus less open to criticism. To do this, he must take as much power as possible into his own hands. This may not work to the detriment of the association's interests. But it reinforces the inactivity of the majority.[9]

In an illuminating study of ten associations in Minnesota, John Tsouderos describes the process of formalization in voluntary associations and the resulting alienation of members. During the early stages of its organization, while there is still enthusiasm arising from a sense of participation in a significant new movement, membership grows rapidly. But as membership grows, it becomes increasingly heterogeneous and the early feeling of intimacy and close cooperation declines. Attendance at meetings and interest in volunteer work falls off. The membership becomes increasingly passive and increasingly distant from the leadership, and some begin to leave the organization. Meanwhile the association's income continues to grow even for a time after membership begins to decline. By the same token, expenditures for administrative staff, office help, and property continue to grow after income declines. In order to cope with declining membership and income, the association requires higher dues and turns more to professional staff. These and other new formal organizational features further alienate the members, who continue to drop out, thus driving the association to still further formalization.[10] This "vicious circle" is not an inevitable development. As Sills's study of the National Foundation for Infantile Paralysis indicates, it can be circumvented.[11] But it is not likely to be avoided unless the tendency toward formalization is clearly recognized. Unfortunately, this formalization occurs frequently, thus frequently reinforcing the inactivity of the majority.

The concentration of executive functions in large, powerful organizations in government and in industry as well as in voluntary associations is a ubiquitous reality of modern civilization. It contributes much to the apathy of modern man regarding public issues, as C. Wright Mills tirelessly contends throughout his book *White Collar*. So overwhelming does this concentration of power appear to the average man that if the unlikely thought of initiating change in the social order occurs to him, he is likely to despair of accomplishing his goal before he even begins.

The organizational necessity for the concentration of executive functions can serve as a source of discouragement also to those who are actively attempting to carry on social action through existing large-scale voluntary associations. Probably most difficult and discouraging would be the obstacles against any attempt to displace established leadership opposed to any activity relating to social action in a thoroughly formalized association with a large, indifferent majority, where the leadership was determined to maintain its grip on the organization. Perhaps in most such cases it would be better to look for other channels through which to express social concern! But even an ordinary large-scale association, relatively sincerely attempting to promote democratic participation, presents formidable obstacles to anyone wishing to initiate a new line of action. Its sheer size, its complexity, the sluggishness of its democratic processes, and the inertia and indifference of the majority of its members all work against such efforts and discourage any such attempts.

To be sure, the concentration of executive functions in the large association need not be entirely a source of discouragement to those concerned about social action. This concentration of power offers upon occasion extraordinary opportunities for the exertion of considerable influence by those who will take initiative and will work assiduously for specific, limited social changes. A few committed people working together, or even an energetic individual, can exercise an influence far out of proportion to their numbers. Although such opportunities are available, motivation for social action must already exist if they are to be exploited. The structure of large-scale voluntary associations works effectively against such motivation.

As a factor affecting motivation for social action, the structure of associations, with the tendency toward concentration of executive functions, cannot be adequately evaluated apart from an understanding of the specific goals to which associations are committed. Two basic questions arise in this connection: (1) To what extent are existing associations already committed to some form of social action? Those that are so committed can be expected not only to offer opportunities for social action to people who are already motivated in that direction but also to encourage some people to begin engaging in social action. (2) To what extent are associations which are not committed to social action sufficiently flexible to accept some impulse toward social action initiated by the membership? The answer to this question depends very much, of course, upon the nature of each specific association. Nevertheless, some tentative general conclusions can be presented in answer to it. Therefore, I shall attempt to answer this second question in a general manner before trying to deal with both in a more specific manner.

Inflexibility of Established Voluntary Associations

It has been found that, in general, voluntary associations have very little flexibility in revising basic goals and purposes once these have become established. There has apparently been very little systematic study of this matter and there is very little concrete evidence available to support this conclusion. But a number of observers have noted the inflexibility of established association goals.[12] Apparently they base their conclusions primarily on experience and keen observation.

In his very thorough study of voluntary associations connected with the Tennessee Valley Authority, Philip Selznick noted the tendency toward inflexibility in associations, once their goals and procedures had become established or institutionalized.

> The systematized commitments of an organization define its character. Day-to-day decision, relevant to the actual problems met in the translation of policy into action, create precedents, alliances, effective symbols, and personal loyalties which transform the organization from a profane, manipulable instrument into something having a sacred status and thus resistant to treatment simply as a means to some external goal. That is why organizations are often cast aside when new goals are sought.[13]

Rose, approaching the matter from a slightly different angle, arrives at a similar conclusion.

> The purposes of associations are as diverse as can be imagined. The only thing they have in common is that the purposes are limited, and almost never will an association act for a purpose different from the original one which brought the members together. The reason is easy to understand: People who have one interest in common will not necessarily have another interest in common, and any effort to act on a second purpose is likely to split the association.[14]

To be sure, voluntary associations are by no means totally inflexible, and some of them exhibit a considerable ability to change. Sills, in discussing this issue, cites several examples of associations that have revised their goals. The Y.M.C.A., for example, was founded in London "to improve the spiritual condition of young men engaged in the drapery and other trades."[15] Today it is a very successful organization fulfilling a social need by providing recreational and athletic facilities, but with very little of its original explicit religious emphasis. The Red Cross, which was founded to provide medical and other help in time of war or national calamity, has broadened its interests to the ongoing problems of public health. Sills correctly predicted that the very vital National Foundation for Infantile Paralysis would find a new goal after having conquered polio.[16] At present, having changed its name to the National Foundation, it continues to raise money through the March of Dimes to help overcome birth defects and arthritis.

But, as Sills indicates, the flexibility of voluntary associations is limited. In each case where an association changed direction it was readily able to justify its change in terms of its original purpose. The Foundation, for example, still focuses attention on a dramatic threat to health, and thus it can continue to count on the virtually complete public sympathy which it has always enjoyed. Its nature has changed, but not very radically. An association like the Y.M.C.A. may adjust gradually to changing situations over a long period of time. But it appears that an association can change abruptly only when it must respond to some threat to its survival. The threat can be either of two basic sorts, or a combination of them: (1) The association's goals may become irrelevant to a changing social environment or (2) the association may achieve its original purpose.[17] But whether the change is gradual or abrupt, it apparently must be consistent with the association's original purpose. Thus, those who wish to employ the resources of existing voluntary associations in order to carry on social action must recognize that they need to keep their activities rather well confined to the existing goals and procedures of the associations.

Goals of Existing Voluntary Associations

With an understanding of the structure of large-scale voluntary associations, and of the tendency for established associations to remain rather inflexible, we are better equipped to discern the extent to which existing associations, given their particular goals and commitments, on the one hand provide openings or opportunities for social action, and on the other hand encourage motivation for social action. The goals of associations reflect and express, of course, the interests of individuals. At the same time, associations play such a prominent role in American society that they unavoidably do much to shape the interests of individuals. How much they do so is impossible to say. But in the publicity they draw, the honors they bestow, the status they grant, and the advantages they gain, they undoubtedly do much to mold the values and interests of individuals. Just how do the goals of existing voluntary associations affect attitudes toward social action?

Our first problem in the attempt to answer this question, a problem of no mean proportion, is to discern the goals of existing associations. Unfortunately, only a few fragmentary and incomplete attempts have been made to analyze the goals, purposes, and commitments of the great array of voluntary associations in the United States or in any particular American community. Various typologies for classifying associations have been developed, but no standard typology has become accepted. Thus it is very difficult to compare the results of various studies. Furthermore, none of the typologies that have come to my attention has been developed in order to reveal the degree of social action to which various associations are committed. The most thorough analysis and classification of the goals of voluntary associations of which I am aware is Sherwood Fox's dissertation, which examines 5,241 associations organized at the national level.[18] But Fox's conclusions, growing out of his interest in how voluntary associations maintain the existing order, do not adequately answer our question concerning the degree to which various types of associations contribute to social action.

Since 1952, when Fox collected his list of associations, more complete data on the great array of national associations of the United States have become available. In 1956 the Gale Research Company first published its *Encyclopedia of American Associations,* with listings of about 6,500 different associations. New editions were published in 1959, in 1961, and in 1964, each with an increased number of listings. The fourth edition, published in 1964, contains 12,950 (8,800 at the national level). It is the most nearly complete and probably the most representative list of associations of national scope now available.[19]

The *Encyclopedia* makes no attempt to analyze or to interpret its data, except to divide the associations into twenty different categories. It gives the name of the association, the address of its headquarters, and varying amounts of additional information, usually including the number of members and staff, and often including excerpts from its statement of purpose. Its classification system was, of course, not designed to reveal the associations' extent of commitment to social action. Even though it does not directly serve our purpose, it at least provides a wealth of information on voluntary associations not available elsewhere, including some indication of their goals, and its classification system does bring some order to the chaotic welter of material that is available. Therefore, using the listing and classification of associations that appears in the 1964 edition, I shall attempt to make some judgments about the goals of existing associations and about their impact upon motivation for social action. My procedure is unscientific and my judgments are impressionistic. Therefore my conclusions are offered very tentatively. I urge the skeptical to check my impressions by surveying the *Encyclopedia* for themselves, or better yet by setting up a research project that will yield more reliable conclusions![20]

Since the *Encyclopedia of Associations* does not indicate how many associations it lists, the table on the following page provides the number of associations included within each category, and the percentage of each type, arranged in order from the category with the largest number of associations to that with the smallest. Such a count fails, of course, to do justice to many important facts about various associations. Some associations, for example, claim less than ten members whereas others have many thousands and even millions of members.

If the *Encyclopedia's* classifications were rearranged according to total memberships, from highest to lowest, their order might well be quite different. Labor unions might head the list. But this arrangement would fail to distinguish between nominal memberships and intensely active memberships, and would fail to do justice to other factors differentiating the associations, such as the extent of their power and influence or the breadth of their interests. Despite the inadequacy of the classification and count given in the table, this data can, nevertheless, when used with some description of the nature of each category and the particular kinds of associations included, help to indicate the extent to which opportunities or encouragement for social action are offered by voluntary associations of national scope.

National Associations of the United States, 1964*

	Number	Percent
Trade, Business, and Commercial Organizations	2,724	31.8
Educational and Cultural Organizations	873	10.2
Health and Medical Organizations	681	8.0
Religious Organizations (not churches or denominations)	648	7.6
Fraternal, Foreign Interest, Nationality, and Ethnic Organizations	587	6.9
Agricultural Organizations and Commodity Exchanges	444	5.2
Scientific, Engineering, and Technical Organizations	403	4.7
Social Welfare Organizations	334	3.9
Greek Letter Societies	327	3.8
Public Affairs Organizations	312	3.6
Hobby and Avocational Organizations	267	3.1
Governmental, Public Administration, Military, and Legal Organizations	243	2.8
Athletic and Sports Organizations	233	2.7
Labor Unions	231	2.7
Veterans, Hereditary, and Patriotic Organizations	173	2.0
Horticultural Organizations	88	1.0
TOTAL	8,568	100.0

* *Encyclopedia of Associations,* Fourth Edition, Vol. 1, *National Organizations of the United States* (Gale Research Company, Detroit, Michigan, 1964). Used by permission.

Omitted for purposes of this table are 147 general organizations not classified, 45 organizations received too late to classify, and 4,195 chambers of commerce, since these are not only national, but also international, binational, state, and local.

The number of associations of each type is not given in the *Encyclopedia* itself, but in an undated news release mailed by the Gale Research Company upon request. Not including chambers of commerce, the *Encyclopedia* lists 8,760 associations.

Calculations of percentages are my own.

It is apparent from a glance at the table that only a small percentage of the organizations listed in the *Encyclopedia of Associations* is directly committed to social action. Most of these are listed as public affairs organizations. This category includes most of the best known and most powerful associations committed to social action. But it also includes numerous associations committed more to research and to education than to social action, along with organizations of the far right, such as the John Birch Society, whose purposes in my judgment do not correspond with the goals of social action.

Other categories contain at best only a scattering of associations devoted to social action. A few of the educational and cultural organizations have interests which could qualify as social action, although their activities are generally noncontroversial. The United Negro College Fund, for example, attempts to expand facilities and opportunities in higher education for a disadvantaged group. Only a few of the associations included among religious organizations are committed to social action since most such religious groups are listed in the public affairs category. Among the agricultural organizations is a surprisingly large group of fifty-four conservation associations. In their attempts to gain commitments from American society to maintain the nation's great natural beauty and its wildlife, they are carrying on a type of social action for the benefit of the public in present and in future generations. Virtually unique among the scientific, engineering, and technical organizations is the Society for Social Responsibility in Science. A few of the social welfare organizations, such as the American Friends Service Committee and the National Urban

League, engage in social action as well as in social welfare activities. Whereas most of the governmental, public administration, military, and legal organizations are professional groups promoting the skills and interests of their members, a very few, such as the American Law Institute which works for clarification of the law "and its better adaptation to social needs" and attempts "to secure the better administration of justice," are involved in social action. Outside of these categories, however, there are, as far as I can see, no associations listed in the *Encyclopedia* that are committed to social action.

All told, judging by the data available in the *Encyclopedia of Associations,* only a small minority of the voluntary associations organized at the national level in the United States— a generous estimate would be no more than 5 percent—is actively committed to social action. Thus only a small minority, through the example of their own activity in which they call upon others to participate, actively stimulate motivation for social action. Of course, participation in such associations is only voluntary, and they can be easily ignored or even condemned by those who are not already favorably disposed toward social action.

To what extent are opportunities for social action available in the great majority of voluntary associations that do not encourage motivation for social action because they are not committed to it? Seldom could it be said with finality that such opportunities are entirely absent from any association if highly imaginative and energetic people attempted to direct its energies toward some form of social action related to its existing goals. But we can say that some associations are apparently amenable to social action and some are not. I shall first mention the categories of associations in the *Encyclopedia* least amenable to social action, not because they are hostile to it, though some are—an interesting topic which I shall not pursue here—but because they effectively exclude it by directing their interests elsewhere.

Certainly the horticultural organizations with their interest in gardening, and the hobby and avocational organizations with 84 associations for fanciers of various kinds of dogs, and with scores more for collectors of various items ranging from old airplanes to cigar bands, are simply irrelevant to social action. Although athletics and sports have sometimes been effective channels for breaking down racial and ethnic barriers, the associations in this category in general are little less irrelevant to social action. Most of the veterans, hereditary, and patriotic organizations are too uncritically devoted to the existing order in the United States or to some imagined ideal order of the past to be amenable to social action. Greek letter societies are interested in sociability, possibly in status, and sometimes in scholastic honors. Although they sometimes become objects of social action when attempts are made to break down their exclusiveness, they seldom if ever become agents of social action. The fraternal organizations—not Greek letter fraternities and sororities—include Masons, Freemasons, Rosicrucians, Odd Fellows, Elks, and Shriners, which sometimes engage in community service, but rarely in social action. They also include life insurance societies or benefit insurance societies irrelevant to social action. The foreign interest, nationality, and ethnic organizations grouped in the same category with fraternal associations might occasionally work for their rights as minority groups, but seem to be interested primarily in preserving the identity and culture of their respective groups and in providing occasions for social contact within the group. All these types of voluntary associations, therefore, making up nearly 20 percent of the total included in the *Encyclopedia,* appear to be among the least responsive to social action.

Most of the religious organizations not already committed to social action, except perhaps those involved in social welfare, are not likely to become amenable to it. Organizations supported financially by the churches would be especially likely to have difficulty in shifting toward social action because the churches in our society function primarily to support the existing social order, and frequently discourage impulses toward social action.[21] On the other hand, interest in social action has increased in recent years in the churches, and new voluntary associations have arisen to implement this concern (listed in the *Encyclopedia* primarily as public affairs organizations). Moreover, most of the major denominations in the United States have official boards or agencies concerned with social education and action, and the National Council of the Churches of Christ in the U.S.A. devotes a large part of its resources to social action. The churches and synagogues constantly preach an ideology of love for other human beings which might well be expressed through social action. Church people who attempt to initiate social action through the churches and through their related voluntary associations, therefore, frequently have possibilities for sympathetic response, although they may have to exert exceptional effort to launch a program of action.

The trade, business, and commercial organizations can be discussed together with the agricultural organizations and commodity exchanges—excluding the conservation groups already mentioned—since their goals are very similar. Together they make up more than 35 percent of the associations listed in the *Encyclopedia*. Membership in such voluntary associations is often not really voluntary, although active participation is likely to be a voluntary matter. For the most part, each of these associations, connected with some particular industry, is intent on promoting its own interests by sharing information within the industry, by cooperative research, by promoting good public relations, by working for legislative advantages, and the like. Such associations are generally backed by strong financial resources and are thus able to wield considerable power in the political as well as in the economic order. Since most of them are thoroughly committed to promoting existing economic enterprises, they are unlikely to respond to social action.[22] However, as they are strategically located in the power structures of American society, they ought to be taken into consideration as possible instruments for social action.

The scientific, engineering, and technical organizations, about 5 percent of the total, perform valuable functions in stimulating the growth of scientific knowledge upon which our social system has become dependent. They share new scientific knowledge, honor outstanding contributors to science, and promote the professional interests of their members. They have virtually no commitment to social action at present, but might be pressed to express concern for the social consequences of vital new scientific discoveries.

The associations listed under the categories of educational and cultural organizations, health and medical organizations, and social welfare organizations together make up more than 20 percent of those listed in the *Encyclopedia*. They make valuable contributions in the fields of health, education, and welfare, but little of their work includes social action since, for the most part, they provide help for individuals rather than work to change social institutions, and since they generally express existing commitments of our society rather than challenge those commitments. Many of these associations, however, especially in the social welfare category, are concerned with providing services to disadvantaged groups and might well be amenable to social action directed toward increasing the commitment of the community to support such work and toward overcoming the underlying social problems that render some people disadvantaged.

Many of the governmental, public administration, military, and legal organizations are professional groupings designed to provide mutual assistance for meeting problems in the job and to promote the professional interests of their members. Since most of these associations are related to occupations which serve the public interest and which deal with public concerns, many of them might well be amenable to initiatives for social action.

Labor unions, among the least voluntary of all voluntary

associations, perform the extremely valuable role of providing a counterbalance to the great economic power of employers who run large business enterprises. They have done much to win a fair proportion of the nation's wealth for laborers. In recent years, however, they have lost much of their thrust toward social action, and most of them are probably no longer very responsive to it. They concentrate on supporting the interests of employees who may be far from disadvantaged. With millions of members and considerable financial resources, labor unions possess great political and economic power. Yet problems created by automation and by increasing leisure concern them directly and urgently. They might welcome energetic, competent initiative that would enable them to deal creatively with such problems.[23]

Impact of Existing Voluntary Associations Upon Social Action

The attempt I have made to discern the goals of existing voluntary associations and to identify the types that are committed to social action and those which might be amenable to initiatives for social action has been sketchy and imprecise. Nevertheless, the conclusion appears inescapable. Only a very small minority of voluntary associations of national scope in the United States are committed to social action and actively encourage participation in it. The great majority have interests and commitments that rather effectively exclude the possibility that they might be persuaded to include some form of social action among their activities. While a rather large minority might be amenable to engaging in social action, few would move in that direction without extremely aggressive prodding.

A more adequate study of the goals of existing voluntary associations would have to include some analysis of associations not only at the national level but at the local level as well, because significant differences could conceivably appear.

Although several community studies have dealt with the goals of local voluntary associations, they have not evaluated these associations for their contributions to social action. But from the limited evidence available, it appears that local voluntary associations have no more interest in social action than those at the national level.[24]

For those who are willing and able to take initiative to seek them out and to work long and hard for small results, opportunities for social action through existing voluntary associations abound. But discouragements abound all the more. The sheer weight of associations' commitments to goals other than social action, combined with their inflexibility and with their tendency toward concentration of executive functions, obscured by the trappings of democracy, all present formidable discouragements even for those who are already well motivated to engage in social action. For those who have little interest in social action, most existing associations do nothing to arouse it.

How is initiative for social action to arise? Although opportunities for social action are plentiful, initiative is scarce. The existing institutions of American society—the economic order, the political order, the family, the voluntary associations, the churches—offer stimulus for social action that falls far short of the needs. Initiative must be taken by individuals. Yet individuals are profoundly influenced by their society, its values and its institutions. By evaluating social action as merely voluntary, American society ensures that it receives very little initiative.

7

Dependence Upon the Job for Income as an Obstacle to Social Action

LIKE THE VOLUNTARY ASSOCIATION, the job is a channel through which social action can be expressed. But unlike the voluntary association, the job is obligatory. Faithful performance in the job is a prime requirement of the American social system, and it is not left to chance. Powerful instruments of social control ensure that the obligation will be performed faithfully. Very rarely does faithful performance in the job include social action, and there are only a few people in American society whose jobs oblige them to promote social action—as, for example, a legislator who has been elected on a reform platform, or a professional official in a voluntary association committed to social action, or an executive in an unusual type of government agency whose functions include social action. Such jobs are rare. Nearly all positions in the occupational system require those who hold them to work at tasks that provide support for the existing social order. Social action is not what most jobholders are hired for. Nevertheless, many people in the United States, especially those who hold executive positions in big business and in government, wield considerable power in their jobs that they *might* use in behalf of social action. The social pressures against their doing so, however, are formidable.

Social Pressures Against Social Action Through the Job

To begin with, some informal voluntary association, some initiating group, would probably be as much a prerequisite for social action through the job as through the voluntary association. Individual effort would probably be insufficient without the stimulus and support of some group meeting outside the work situation to identify problems, to plan and to carry out strategy, and to provide mutual encouragement and sustained effort in the face of delays and opposition. Thus motivation for social action through the job faces in most cases the same disadvantages that confront motivation for social action attempted through the voluntary association. In both cases, social action requires exceptional persistence and effort, and yet is defined in American society as being merely voluntary activity which must be carried on largely or entirely during leisure hours.

In order to engage in social action either through the voluntary association or through the job, a person must raise critical questions about the existing social order. He must present imaginative alternatives designed to achieve a greater degree of justice than existing arrangements allow. He must be willing to press for needed change in the face of opposition. All these activities are likely to be especially difficult in the context of the job. If the individual is to carry on social action in and through his job, he may have to call into question the established and revered goals of the very organization for which he works. Others holding key positions in the organization might well take a dim view of his efforts. Thus a person can only engage in social action through his job with the forthrightness and boldness that social action requires if in the last analysis he is willing to risk the possibility of losing his job, or at least of losing opportunities for promotion.

In modern industrial society, power is increasingly coming to be concentrated in large bureaucratic organizations. Not much power is available outside such organizations. Those most likely to have access to power in their jobs which might be used for social action are those who participate at their jobs in the decision-making processes of large governmental and business bureaucracies. However, both the structure and the goals of these bureaucratic organizations work against the possibility that even their executives might exercise initiative for social action through them. Since power in the bureaucracy is usually concentrated at the top of a hierarchy of authority and status, the majority of its employees, even among the executive ranks, wield little influence in shaping its policies.[1] The lower-ranking executive or technical expert is not without influence. But his influence is likely to be far more effective in implementing established goals than in establishing new goals. He may well feel that effort to initiate movement toward new goals would be so futile that he does not even try. Even those few who occupy top-level positions in bureaucracies may have little freedom to use the power of their organizations for social action even if they should want to. The goals of such organizations are usually too well established in support of the existing order, of which the organizations themselves are formidable elements, for even top management to redirect them.[2]

Perhaps pessimistic judgments are premature because possibilities for social action through the job in bureaucratic organizations are only beginning to be explored. A few years ago the mere suggestion that the job might be used as a channel for social action would have been widely regarded as heretical, especially in business circles. Recently, however, a few businesses have at their own expense set up job-training programs for undereducated people, have established job information centers, have renovated tenements, and have provided free management-consulting services to help Negroes start their own businesses.[3] The fact that these steps can for the most part be seen as consistent with the self-interest of the corporations does not prevent them from qualifying as social action. They involve a departure from the established commitments of the businesses and they are moves in the direction of greater justice. Once such programs become well accepted, however, they will no longer be matters for social action.

It is remotely conceivable that those extraordinarily dynamic and powerful bureaucratic organizations, the corporations, might become more and more involved in providing initiatives in social action. Already, under the impetus of increasingly complex technology and production processes, corporations have been forced into increasingly long-range planning.[4] They might come to see more fully than they do already that their health depends directly upon the health of the total environment in which they live. They might do a great deal to overcome racial injustice, poverty, and urban blight in domestic affairs, and they might work for peace in international relations if they could see such activities as directly relevant to their own drive for growth and for autonomy.[5] They could not engage in such activities, of course, without the cooperation of the Government, but they might win this cooperation by their own highly creative initiative.

The task of social action, however, constantly calls for new ventures that involve new risks. This is true both for organizations and for individuals. But organizations tend to resist and to resent pressures upon them to take risks that they do not perceive as essential for achieving their basic, established goals. Few organizations that are not already committed to social action are likely to welcome pressure, especially from within, to become involved in social action. Even if certain forms of social action should be relevant to their basic interests, they are likely to perceive them, at least initially, as risky. Thus the individual who attempts to initiate social action through his job must expect opposition and must be willing to risk the possibility of losing his job or opportunities for promotion.

Very few Americans, however, are willing to accept this risk. Indeed, very seldom does it even enter the minds of most people that any responsibility of theirs should require them to risk their jobs. Any such thought is simply eliminated from the realm of consideration. There are two fundamental reasons for our unwillingness to risk our jobs and for our common failure even to consider the possibility: (1) We are primarily dependent upon our jobs for our income and (2) we are primarily dependent upon our jobs for our status. In short, we are dependent upon the job both for fundamental biological needs and for fundamental psychological needs. I shall deal with each of these factors in turn in this chapter and in the next.

Income from Work as a Means of Social Control

Perhaps it seems all too obvious to mention that the great majority of Americans do not wish to risk the loss of their jobs because the earnings that they gain from their work are their primary source of income for the necessities of life. But this fact needs to be mentioned precisely because it is so obvious. It is so obvious that it is taken for granted, and its influence in shaping our attitude toward the social order is generally overlooked. Our dependence upon income from work is a basic element in our system of social control by which our loyal performance at the job is ensured and our support for the existing order gained. The more readily such a fundamental fact is overlooked, the more completely it is taken for granted, and the more unconscious people are of its operation in their lives, then the more effective it is as an instrument of social control. In societies where an aristocratic class uses slave labor, the means of social control enforcing the obligation to work are much more overtly coercive, and they are not very readily taken for granted. Dangerously disruptive resentment is likely to arise against their patent injustice. There is little sense of injustice, though, aroused against instruments of social control enforcing the obligation to work in American society, except where there is high unemployment or inequality of job opportunity. So readily do Americans accept as a normal and natural part of life that they are directly dependent for their survival upon the income that they receive from work, and so inherently right does this system seem to them, that this instrument of social control is highly effective.

But income from work is effective as an instrument of social control not simply because the general principle of working for a living is almost universally and unquestionably accepted. It is effective also because several presently prevailing customs and social arrangements, connected with the receiving and spending of personal income in the United States, help to make it so. Closer examination of the sources and the uses of the American people's income will clarify how effectively income from work operates as an instrument of social control, ensuring performance of job obligations, and hence providing support for the existing order and hindrance to social action.

Income from Earnings in the United States

The fact that all but a small minority of families in the United States are dependent for the bulk of their income upon the earnings that they gain from the work of the family breadwinner(s) is so well known that it hardly needs documentation. The clear picture that statistics can give us, however, is more useful than a vague generalization. In 1959, the latest year for which complete statistics are available, 92 percent of the 45.1 million families in the nation had income from earnings. The remaining 8 percent do not concern us here since they did not have jobs that they might have used for social action. Of those who had earnings, 57 percent were totally dependent upon their jobs for their income. But a sizable 43 percent had other income as well.[6] To what extent were they dependent upon their jobs for their income?

The 17.8 million families who had earnings and other income in 1959 received an average or a mean total income of $8,063, of which $6,827, or 84.7 percent was earnings. Although the average other income was thus $1,236, the median other income was only $650, indicating that few people had very large amounts of other income. Indeed, only some 4.0 million families out of the 17.8 million in this group received $1,500 or more of other income, and only 1.5 million received $3,000 or more of other income. Only in the income brackets under $4,000 did the average family receive more than 25 percent of its income from sources other than earnings. Undoubtedly many of these families were receiving relief payments or Social Security benefits. Even in the highest income bracket—those with total incomes of $15,000 or more—the average family received only 19 percent of its income from sources other than earnings.[7]

Thus it is apparent that nearly all the families in the United States who have some member working in the world of occupation are overwhelmingly dependent upon earnings for their income, and we can hardly expect to find much willingness to risk loss of the job. The sole source of income for more than half of all American families is the job. Those with incomes under $4,000 who receive more than 25 percent of their income from sources other than earnings live so close to starvation that they can ill afford to risk losing their small earnings. Moreover, if they are not so discouraged that they have lost interest in everything, they are likely to be more interested in survival than in social action. When even the average family with mixed types of income totaling $15,000 or more has $23,000 of earnings to only $4,500 of other income,[8] we can hardly expect to find among them much willingness to risk loss of the job. A family accustomed to a $28,000 style of life is not likely to be willing to adjust to a $4,500 style of life. Of course, a $4,500 income from sources other than earnings usually presupposes savings or investments worth over $100,000. The security provided by these savings might enable a man to risk losing his job. I suspect, however, that one who has become accustomed to the reassurance and to the prospective spending provided by such a backlog of saving would be most reluctant to surrender any sizable part of it. Moreover, the man who has lost a high-paying job is likely to have difficulty in finding an equivalent replacement for it. But in any case, people at these higher income levels are likely to want to preserve the existing order rather than to introduce changes.

In addition to the 45.1 million families in the United States, there were, in 1959, 13.2 million unrelated individuals fourteen years of age and older. Many of these people, without the pressure of family responsibilities, might well have a freedom to risk their jobs that people with families to support could not readily have. Of the unrelated individuals, 6.2 million or 47 percent had income from earnings only, and their mean income was $2,747; 2.5 million or 19 percent had earnings and other income. For this group mean earnings were $3,081 and mean other income was $845, indicating that there was very little lack of dependence upon the job.[9] Probably among people with such small earnings few would have the initiative or drive to engage in social action. Moreover, jobs producing such little income are not likely to be effective channels for social action. It is apparent that very few unrelated individuals would have the drive or the opportunities to engage in social action through the job, even if they happened to have the interest.

Immediate Dependence
Upon Regular Income from Earnings

Not only is work the sole or primary source of income for the great majority of Americans, but also most Americans are directly dependent for their *immediate* necessities and desires upon the regular income that they receive from their daily work. For most, the regular rhythm of the weekly, biweekly, or monthly paycheck is essential to maintain the family standard of living, whether it be bare subsistence level or whether it be the affluence of modern suburbia. This fundamental reality of

American life makes it extremely difficult for most Americans to take any risk with their jobs. They are especially unlikely to risk their jobs in some enterprise, such as social action, which is directed toward the benefit of others, and which promises little obvious, immediate benefit to themselves.

For the wage laborer during the early 1920's, there was only a narrow margin between his weekly paycheck and his family's needs. When in labor disputes employers proposed year-end profit-sharing schemes, they failed to arouse much interest among the workers because they had not recognized the urgent need of laborers for the weekly paycheck to meet immediate obligations. When even a slight, unexpected expenditure, like new shoes for the baby, could necessitate a man's walking to work instead of taking the customary streetcar, the narrow margin between well-being and deprivation became apparent.[10] Also apparent was the relentless pressure that a man felt to hold his job.

One might suppose that since the real income of most Americans has increased substantially over that of the 1920's,[11] the pressure to hold one's job during the 1960's would not be quite so relentless. To be sure, there are still great numbers of Americans who live in poverty, and for them the pressure has certainly not diminished. One might think, however, that for the majority whose income has risen above the bare subsistence level, and for whom greater savings should be possible, immediate dependence upon the regular paycheck would become a thing of the past. But this has not happened. The face is that along with the rise in real wages has gone a steady expansion and diffusion in the number and variety of commodities that are considered essential for normal, everyday living in the United States. Yesterday's luxuries become today's necessities. The Lynds in their 1925 study of Middletown provide an impressive list of goods and services that had come to be regarded since the 1890's as virtually essential.

> *In the home*—furnace, running hot and cold water, modern sanitation, electric appliances ranging from toasters

to washing machines, telephone, refrigeration, green veg-
etables and fresh fruit all the year round, greater variety
of clothing, silk hose and underwear, commercial pressing and cleaning of clothes, commercial laundering or
use of expensive electrical equipment in the home, cos-
metics, manicuring, and commercial hair-dressing.

In spending leisure time—movies . . . , automobile . . . ,
phonograph, radio, more elaborate children's playthings,
more club dues for more members of the family, . . .
more formal dances and banquets, . . . cigarette smoking
and expensive cigars.

In education—high school and college (involving longer
dependence of children), many new incidental costs such
as entrance to constant school athletic contests.[12]

During the depression there was only a temporary curtail-
ment in expenditures for these new items. Many of the new
conveniences had become well established as part of the American style of life, and the durable goods continued in use,
although not replaced with new equipment. Notable among
these was the automobile. Although purchases of new automobiles in Middletown dropped rather sharply between 1929
and 1933, automobile registrations dipped only slightly, and
gasoline sales fell by only 4 percent.[13] With economic recovery
in the latter 1930's the public appetite for consumer goods
again became apparent. Even during the great national emergency of World War II when we congratulated ourselves on
pouring all our strength into the war effort, the insatiable desire for consumer goods was not to be denied. From 1940 to
1945, consumer spending in the United States increased from
$122.5 billion to $145.2 billion, an increment of about $23 bil-
lion. During the following five peacetime years, the increment
was not strikingly larger—a little under $38 billion. The use of
resources for consumer goods was justified as essential for
maintaining civilian morale![14] Other expensive durable goods
have been added to the American appetite since World War II.

Among these are air conditioners, power mowers, freezers, de-
humidifiers, food-waste disposers, and dishwashers. The outstanding favorite has been television which became available
to the public only after the war and is now a prominent feature
in virtually every American home.

While the real income of Americans has grown impressively
since the 1920's, increasingly larger proportions of this income
have gone to taxes and hence have not been available for
coveted consumer items. In 1929 taxes paid by individuals and
families to federal, to state, and to local governments took
about 10 percent of personal income. In 1966 the proportion
was about 24 percent. In addition, employees' contributions to
social insurance taxes rose from about .3 percent of personal
income in 1929 to about 3.1 percent in 1966.[15]

In *The Organization Man,* Whyte revealed how relentless is
the drain upon family income in affluent modern suburbia. The
suburban style of life requires a rather substantial income as a
bare minimum—between $4,800 and $5,200 back in 1956 when
wages and prices were considerably lower—and the minimum
standard steadily shifts upward as neighbors and contempo-
raries expand their consumption. Suburbanites confidently expect that their income and their spending will steadily increase
over the years as the family breadwinner works his way up in
his chosen career, and as the growing family fulfills its expectations for an increasingly gracious style of living.[16] As Parkinson puts it:

> Expenditure rises to meet income. Parkinson's Second Law
> . . . is a matter of everyday experience, manifest as soon
> as it is stated, as obvious as it is simple. When the in-
> dividual has a raise in salary, he and his wife are prone to
> decide how the additional income is to be spent; so much
> on an insurance policy, so much to the savings bank, so
> much in a trust fund for the children. They might just
> as well save themselves the trouble, for no surplus ever
> comes into view. The extra salary is silently absorbed,

leaving the family barely in credit and often, in fact, with a deficit which has actually increased. Individual expenditure not only rises to meet income but tends to surpass it, and probably always will.[17]

Few people in our consumption-oriented society, except for the very wealthiest, can escape this relentless drain on their income.

Not only do most Americans spend their income as fast as they receive it. More and more they are, in effect, spending their income before they receive it. Whyte described a growing tendency for suburbanites to buy on credit rather than save for expensive major items, and to arrange for payments in regular monthly installments. They seem to be little concerned that they are paying an interest rate of 10 or 12 percent, since their preoccupation is to have a regular monthly budget without any disturbing fluctuations. Even in meeting emergencies, they expect to float loans from the banks that can be met in monthly payments.[18] Whyte found that among the younger couples of Park Forest

> the median equity in savings deposits, bonds, and stocks is about $700 to $800. The median amount of loan money outstanding: $1,000.[19]

With a sizable burden of debt placing a steady drain on the regular paycheck, and with little inclination to avoid the habit of debt-financing, we can expect to find little independence from the regular wage or salary, and, accordingly, little willingness to take risks in the job.

Consumer Credit

One of the most striking developments on the financial scene in the United States during the last several decades has been the enormous expansion of consumer installment credit or debt. At the end of 1929 consumer installment debt outstanding amounted to 4.2 percent of disposable personal income. At the end of 1966 it amounted to 14.8 percent. This proportion went as high as 7.2 percent in 1940, contracted sharply during the war years to 1.5 percent in 1944, and has been expanding nearly every year since with only occasional slight contractions.[20] Thus, after the abnormal years of the depression and of World War II, consumer installment debt as a proportion of disposable personal income is now more than 3½ times as large as it was in 1929.

The annual rate at which Americans repay their installment debt has increased somewhat less dramatically. In 1929 repayments on installment debt took 6.5 percent of disposable personal income in the United States,[21] and in 1966 repayments took a record high of 14.4 percent of disposable income[22]— more than double the percentage taken in 1929. In 1929 the amount of installment debt repayments was about 50 percent greater than the amount of installment debt outstanding at the end of the year. In 1966 the amount of debt outstanding was slightly larger than the year's repayments. The quantity of debt outstanding at any one time surpassed the quantity of debt repaid annually for the first time in 1965. This indicates that the length of the repayment period has been increasing, and that on the average it now slightly exceeds two years.

The national income statistics revealing the growth of installment credit in these two respects—debt outstanding and debt repaid—indicate somewhat different problems for social action in each case. The growth of debt outstanding, which has clearly been the greater of the two since 1929, probably reflects a largely conscious assumption by great numbers of Americans that the economy will remain sufficiently dependable to enable them to meet sizable debt obligations well into the future. It probably also reflects a largely unconscious willingness to become very closely tied to the job—and a largely unconscious unwillingness to be open to social action through the job. On the other hand, the growth of repayments on installment debt more clearly indicates the proportion of their current income that Americans are willing to commit to the repayment of debt. The larger this proportion, the less likely they are to be able to provide the sort of savings that could help provide a cushion against the loss of the job.

Increasingly, the assumption that consumption need not be postponed until desired items can be purchased out of savings has taken hold in American society. Apparently, once adopted, the habit of installment buying is likely to be relied upon more and more heavily. The median installment debt outstanding of spending units with debt increased from $280 in 1952 to $850 in 1966. Moreover, the proportion of spending units in the United States carrying installment debt has increased markedly —from 38 percent in early 1952 to 49 percent in early 1966.[23] Younger adults, especially those who are married and have young children, are much more likely than older people to assume installment debt, to carry large quantities in relation to their income, and to shoulder long-term debts.[24] Apparently the habit of installment credit financing—and its accompanying tendency to encourage the habit of loyalty to the job—is becoming well established among younger people in American society who might otherwise during these somewhat more formative years be more open to the possibilities for social action through the job.

In addition to consumer installment debt, Americans maintain a good deal of noninstallment debt, which consists of single-payment loans, charge accounts, and service credit. Noninstallment debt outstanding at the end of any year has since 1929 varied little from 3 to 4 percent of disposable personal income except during the war years in 1943 and 1944 when it contracted to as little as 2 percent.[25] On a quarterly basis from June 1966 to June 1967 it varied between 3.6 and 3.9 percent.[26] This figure may appear at first glance to be insignificant in comparison with installment debt. But payment of noninstallment debt can seldom be postponed for much longer than a month. Most of it must be paid as soon as the monthly paycheck arrives. Even assuming, however, that on the average it could be spread out over two months, noninstallment debt would be six times as large in proportion to the monthly paycheck as it is to the yearly salary, and Americans would be paying out on the average between 20 and 25 percent of the monthly paycheck as soon as it came in to meet debt of this type. For many Americans the proportion must be much larger. Such payments are in addition to installment payments, and to payments for rent or mortgage. With little cash left, many Americans must perpetually resort to their charge accounts to meet current needs. Having spent much of their monthly salary in advance, they experience a small additional pressure keeping them dependent upon regular income from their jobs.

Mortgage Debt

Since 1929, mortgage debt outstanding in the United States has doubled in relation to disposable personal income. At the end of 1929, the total mortgage debt outstanding on 1- to 4-family nonfarm homes amounted to $18.9 billion, which was 22.0 percent of disposable personal income. At the end of 1966 the amount of such debt outstanding was $225.4 billion, 44.6 percent of disposable income.[27] The payments that Americans make, however, in order to retire their mortgage debt do not amount to a very large proportion of the total national disposable income. The proportion was 6.0 percent in 1964.[28] Of course, some people make rental payments rather than mortgage payments, and some own their homes outright. In early 1966, 30 percent of nonfarm families rented their homes, and 62 percent owned their homes. Of those who owned their homes 58 percent had mortgage debt.[29] Thus 36% of the nonfarm families made all the mortgage payments on nonfarm homes. Therefore, although payments on mortgage debt do not take a very large proportion of national disposable income, they do take a rather large proportion of the disposable income of those who have mortgage debt—probably an average somewhere near 20 percent.[30]

The increase in mortgage debt, of course, does not mean a proportional increase in financial burdens for Americans. For most people the alternative to mortgage payments is rental payments. To be sure, mortgage payments tend to run somewhat higher. In early 1966 the median monthly mortgage payment for nonfarm families with mortgage debt was $90, while for those families who paid rent, the median payment was $70.[31] Furthermore, the housing expenditures of the mortgage payers above the rent payers are further increased by expenses for property taxes and for maintenance and repairs. Moreover, the approximately 34 percent of American spending units who carried mortgage debt in 1960 was much larger than the approximately 19 percent who did so in 1940.[32]

Only partly because it is more expensive does mortgage debt help to keep Americans more closely dependent upon regular income from their jobs than would the necessity for paying rent. Since mortgage debt is ordinarily repaid over a long period of time, it requires a long-term commitment to gaining steady income from the job. A person is most unlikely to make such a commitment with any thought of risking his job. To be sure, if loss of the job should occur, it would be painful for either the mortgage payer or the rent payer if he should be forced to seek other housing arrangements. But terminating a rental arrangement is ordinarily quite simple, whereas selling a house can be very complicated. Moreover, people who own their homes are more likely to become emotionally attached to them. On the other hand, some people with mortgages have sufficient equity in their homes that they could gain funds in case of emergency by refinancing their mortgages. Here home ownership, even with mortgage debt, might be an advantage for social action.

In recent years, however, Americans have begun to use the equity they have accumulated in their homes to finance current spending.

After moving in close consonance with new housing construction for over a decade following World War II, mortgage debt formation started to exceed the value of residential building in 1958. Since 1960, the gap between the two series has widened dramatically, from less than $2 billion to some $10 billion in 1963. This excess of new mortgage debt formation over the value of new residential building represents, in effect, a flow of cash to the personal sector for non-real estate uses.[33]

In view of the heavy emphasis placed upon consumption in the United States, and in view of the fact that the installment debt burden is already quite heavy, it is not surprising that the vast amount of equity in 1- to 4-family nonfarm homes, which remains well over $200 billion,[34] is being converted into funds for consumer expenditures. Mortgage debt can be repaid in smaller installments, over a longer period of time, and with a lower annual rate of interest than can consumer installment debt. Since mortgage debt involves such a long-term commitment—in 1963 the average repayment term was 28 years for existing homes and 31 years for new homes[35]—the use of mortgage debt as a source of funds for consumption may come to exercise increasing influence in keeping Americans tied to their jobs.

Saving

Personal saving in the United States, aside from fluctuations in times of war and depression, has remained remarkably constant during the present century.[36] From 1950 to 1966 personal saving never dropped below 4.9 percent nor rose above 7.6 percent of disposable personal income. A trend toward somewhat smaller personal savings may be developing, however, for since 1959 the proportion has been no higher than 5.8 percent.[37]

But while saving has remained basically stable, there have been marked changes in the forms that saving has taken.

> No change among forms of personal saving is more spectacular than the rise in the share of "tied" saving, i.e., the forms of saving which do not depend on a decision of the saver and those which once begun must be carried through to the termination of the contract, often over a period of several decades, unless part of the savers' contributions are to be lost.[38]

Two of the major forms of "tied" or "contractual" saving are life insurance and pension funds. In 1929 these types of saving made up 21.5 percent of total personal saving in the United States, and in 1960 they made up 50.7 percent—a proportion nearly two and a half times as great. As saving in contractual forms requiring uninterrupted payments has increased, saving in liquid forms, which would be readily available in case of emergency, has decreased.[39]

Thus the presently developing and the presently prevailing patterns of saving in the United States, as well as those of spending and financing, are keeping Americans closely dependent upon regular income from their jobs. The fact that saving in the form of liquid assets has been giving way to saving in contractual forms also helps to ensure that few people will have financial resources to strengthen them to take risks in their jobs for the sake of social action—even in the unlikely event that they should be willing to jeopardize their savings for this purpose.

Pensions

There is a far more direct and effective way in which pensions keep people tied to their jobs than the fact that pensions require saving in contractual form, thus placing a claim on regular income from the job. Pension funds, at least in the private sector of the economy, are accumulated not only through deductions from the wages or salaries of employees but also through far larger contributions from employers. Of the total amount contributed to pension funds in 1966, about 89 percent was provided by employer contributions.[40] In general, employees can gain a right to the money set aside for them by the employer—that is, their pension becomes "vested" —only after a rather long period of faithful service to the company, the period varying widely in individual cases. The fact that engaging in social action could involve the danger not only of losing the job but also of losing with it any claim to the employer's large contributions to the pension fund could exercise considerable influence in weakening possibilities for the impulse toward social action in the job.

During the last generation private pension funds have grown spectacularly in the United States. In 1940 private pension and deferred profit-sharing plans covered 4.1 million workers and had reserves of $2.4 billion. By the end of 1965 the pension plans' reserves had expanded to $85.4 billion and the number of workers covered had risen to 25.4 million.[41] It has been estimated that reserves will reach $200 billion by 1980 and that the number of workers covered will by then be 42 million.[42] Growing numbers of people have come to enjoy the security of increasingly adequate pensions and at the same time they have come to experience a new pressure toward loyal performance in the job. The extent of this pressure depends in a crucial way upon the vesting provisions included in the pension plans.

Only a small percentage of pension plans allow for vesting before an employee has served his company for 10 years. About half require 15 years, and many require longer. Most, either in addition or instead, require attainment of a minimum age rarely less than 40 and which may be as high as 55 or 60.[43] Where attainment of an age is required for vesting, employers frequently avoid hiring older workers.[44] Although vesting provisions of pension plans are becoming more liberal, and pressure for greater liberalization continues,[45] pensions will probably remain for some decades to come an important factor keeping some people tied to their jobs and thus unwilling or reluctant to take the risks involved in social action through the job.

Concern for Income vs. Concern for Social Action

Since most Americans are so closely dependent upon the regular weekly or monthly income from their jobs, it is hardly surprising that they rarely take the risks necessary for carrying on social action through their jobs, and apparently seldom give serious consideration to the possibility. The high value that Americans place upon accumulation of a wide range of consumer items and upon owning their homes, and their willingness to take on increasingly larger quantities of debt in order that they might possess these things as soon as possible, commits large proportions of their regular income in advance to meeting their regular debt payments. Even their saving has increasingly taken the form of regular contractual payments which they cannot interrupt without losing past savings. These commitments, in addition to continuing requirements to spend constantly for such pressing needs as food, clothing, utilities, travel, medical services, and other items, leave Americans little freedom from the regular income that their jobs provide. They are closely dependent upon their jobs, and this dependence is increased if they have unvested pension money accumulating.

To be sure, some people in the United States enjoy a great deal of freedom from dependence upon the job. Many avoid contracting installment debt, or contract very little only occasionally. A large proportion of homeowners has no mortgage debt. Later in their careers employees may have vested pension rights. A few people have large savings and a few enjoy independent income in addition to their earnings. Single people and married people without children may have less urgent demands upon their income. Let each man, from his own pattern of income and expenditure, judge for himself the extent of his freedom for social action!

Unfortunately, even where an individual enjoys considerable freedom from dependence upon the job for income, he is likely to be reluctant to risk giving up earnings to which he has become accustomed. We can achieve a clear commitment to social action through the job only by accepting a serious threat to the security of our earnings.

8

Dependence Upon the Job for Status as an Obstacle to Social Action

THE CONCERN about status which American culture fosters, like the desire for income which it promotes, works effectively to thwart interest in social action through the job. Whereas the desire for income can be gauged reasonably well by readily available statistics regarding income and spending in the United States, concern about status is a complex psychological phenomenon which eludes identification and observation. The drive for status cannot be separated from the drive for income, and both are inextricably intertwined with all sorts of desires for survival, security, comfort, pleasure, power, self-realization, and the like. For our purposes here, however, concern about status can be understood adequately at a commonsense level as an inner drive which includes all these kinds of desires, and which is characterized especially by the urge to achieve standing, to "get ahead," to win prestige, recognition, admiration, and respect in the mainstream of American culture.

Status, like income, is obtained in the United States primarily through the job. Our drive for status impels us to take on existing occupational roles, which, almost without exception, require us to employ our energies in providing rather uncritical support for the existing social order. To press for social action in the job is to disturb the expectations of those who have power to hire and to fire. The desire for status is seldom compatible with an interest in using the job as a channel for social action. Thus, concern about status creates a formidable obstacle against motivation for social action through the job. Moreover, those who are preoccupied with the status that their jobs provide them are not likely to confine their preoccupation to the job situation. They are likely to carry it into their voluntary activities as well.

Extent of Preoccupation with Status

To what extent does concern about status in the United States undermine motivation for social action? Although a great deal of sociological research has been devoted to exploring the status system in the United States, none, as far as I know, has dealt directly with the way in which concern about status affects motivation for social action. We must rely, therefore, upon indirect evidence.

It is my assumption that the more people are preoccupied with striving to gain or to maintain status according to the standards prevailing in our culture, the less they are likely to become interested in social action. Some good evidence is available to support this assumption. One study indicated that upwardly mobile people—among whom we would expect to find especially high preoccupation with status—tend to act more cautiously and more conservatively than socially stable people.[1] They are likely to feel that their newly won status claims are not fully established. Even after they have won improved occupational positions warranting higher status, they are likely to have difficulty in changing their style of life to ingratiate themselves with the more prestigeful group to which they aspire.[2] Apparently, the sense of insecurity experienced by such people often leads them to avoid any activity that would jeopardize their new status. Social action, which calls for a spirit of adventure, and for criticism of the very social system through which the upwardly mobile gain their coveted status, is unlikely to become a possibility for them.

To be sure, striving for status can sometimes help to provide impetus for social action. This is true especially for disadvantaged people who are attempting to improve their lot. But the disadvantaged individual would probably find it easier to concentrate on improving only his own position. The laborer with ability to organize a union, for example, could probably enter management ranks with less effort and risk than founding the union would require. While social action may not always be incompatible with concern about one's own status, rarely are the two likely to be in complete harmony. Ordinarily, taking initiative in social action is an especially difficult and uncertain way of gaining status—especially status as evaluated by the prevailing standards in American culture. At any rate, for those privileged people who have readiest access in their jobs to power that might be used in social action, it is probably safe to assume that the more they are concerned about their status, the less likely they are to initiate social action through their jobs.

Therefore the present chapter focuses on the following question: To what extent are people in the United States preoccupied with gaining or maintaining position in the status system of American society? Since sociologists during the last generation or so have been producing studies of social stratification in prodigious quantities, it might appear that this question would be easy to answer. There are, however, as far as I know, no studies which attempt to measure precisely the extent of Americans' preoccupation with status. This lack is understandable in view of the enormous difficulties that would be involved in finding clear, undisputable, observable measures of preoccupation with status. Much of the literature in social stratification, to be sure, gives the impression that nearly everyone in the United States is intensely concerned with his status in relation to others, and is constantly striving either to improve his social standing or to justify his failure to do so.[3] This impression may well result from a zeal to correct illusions fostered by the American ideology of equality and should probably be treated with some skepticism. Reissman provides a cautionary note:

> Not everybody lives the class life with the same intensity. At one extreme, class can be an all-pervasive reality that burrows into all personal calculations and conceptions. At the other extreme, there are those who can take class or leave it alone.[4]

Apparently the evidence is not sufficiently clear at present to enable us to discern with any precision the extent of preoccupation with status in our society.

At least, however, it can be said that there is in American society a built-in bias toward concern with status. The basic point that I shall argue throughout the rest of this chapter is that functional requirements of our society, and especially of its occupational system, create a continuing pattern of preoccupation with status. Just how great this preoccupation is cannot be stated in precise terms. But it appears to be great enough to interfere profoundly with motivation for social action.

Functional Requirement for Preoccupation with Status

A large proportion of the occupational roles necessary for the functioning of our highly industrial, technological, bureaucratized society are extremely difficult and demanding, and require for their performance a high degree of technical competence. American society generally recruits personnel for most of its occupational roles not from some hereditary elite but from the society at large. The principle that occupations should be distributed according to proven competence is almost universally accepted,[5] and this principle is borne out roughly and approximately in practice.

There is a strong tendency, to be sure, for our society to

gain personnel for the higher, more responsible positions from the higher social classes, that is, from families that already occupy such positions.[6] But this does not necessarily mean that people from privileged families do not have to prove their competence. They may have relatively easy access to opportunities to prove their competence; they are likely to develop their abilities more fully, since they receive higher education as a matter of course; and they are likely to possess other valuable, but intangible assets, such as a sense of self-confidence. In general, though, people of higher social class background must still prove their competence to fill responsible occupational positions. There has never developed a hereditary aristocracy to control the economic and political life of the United States. To be sure, during the early period of industrialization in the United States family ownership and control of the large, new industrial firms was not uncommon. But by the turn of the twentieth century, professionally trained personnel were being increasingly employed at the higher levels of industry, and with few exceptions, professional managers, chosen basically for their competence, now occupy the top positions in the big corporations.[7]

How are people motivated to seek the demanding occupational roles which require considerable training and which call for the shouldering of burdensome responsibilities? American society, like other societies, in general offers its highest rewards for the occupations that impose the heaviest responsibilities and demand the greatest competence. The correlation between high responsibility and high reward is approximate rather than exact, but the two seem to be closely related in most societies, and anomalies tend to disappear in the long run,[8] although there may remain injustices in that differentiation of rewards may well be greater than the differentiation of functions requires.[9]

One of the major rewards, and perhaps the chief reward that every society has to dispense, is that of status. It appears that a sense of self-esteem, which depends primarily upon evaluations of the self by others—upon the status that others grant the self—is a basic need of all human beings. To the extent that our total social system gains the power to influence individuals and families in setting the criteria by which they are evaluated, thus far does it exercise power in granting or in withholding status. Thus far can it make or break self-esteem. Thus far does it gain influence over behavior. A person need not be dependent, at least not fully dependent, upon the total social system for the criteria by which his status is determined. He might receive the status that is most important to him from some smaller social unit with values different from those of the prevailing culture. But the source of the individual's status cannot easily be divorced from the total social system in the United States.[10]

In general, competent performance in responsible occupational positions not only provides roughly corresponding rewards in status in the United States but also provides possibilities for advancement to still more responsible positions and still higher status. Thus the American social system contains a built-in bias toward preoccupation with status. Indeed, such preoccupation is a functional necessity in the United States because the society's more demanding roles could probably not be filled with competent personnel unless many people were striving to improve their status.

Our social system could hardly succeed in granting high status for its most responsible and demanding occupational roles unless it also succeeded in granting low status for its least-demanding occupational roles. A wide variety of low-responsibility, low-skill, and therefore low-status jobs must be performed if our social system is to continue to function. How are people motivated to fill such positions? Although some occupations grant very low status, the positive although slight approval they command is for most people clearly preferable to the condemnation that results from failure to work.[11] This condemnation prevails even if such failure results from conditions beyond the individual's control.[12]

By exerting the highly effective pressure of granting or withholding status, our social system makes it obligatory for almost all able-bodied adult males under retirement age to hold some job or occupation. Only for those seeking high status does it become obligatory to seek the more demanding, more responsible positions. But status is a vitally important consideration even in the least prestigious occupations. In American society, where the more demanding occupational positions are obtained largely through individual ability and effort, with approximately corresponding rewards in status, and where failure to work is punished by strong social disapproval, it can be expected that a good deal of preoccupation with status— conscious or unconscious—prevails.

Structural Changes Affecting Status
in the United States

Over the last 120 to 150 years, the great structural changes wrought in American society by industrialization have brought about greatly increased class and status differentiations, have upset earlier criteria for status, and undoubtedly have increased preoccupation with status. Present patterns of preoccupation with status can best be understood in the light of these far-reaching structural changes.

During the early part of the nineteenth century, American society consisted primarily of independent entrepreneurs. It has been estimated that during the decade of 1820 to 1830 four fifths of the Americans who worked (excluding slaves) owned their own means of livelihood.[13] Most of these were farmers. Even if this estimate is excessively high, the middle stratum of independent, property-owning entrepreneurs was a conspicuous majority, and their style of life became the basis for an ideology of individual achievement which continues to prevail today.[14] Those who had no property could reasonably hope to obtain some. They were encouraged by the fact that little capital was required to start a viable, small, urban business in a world of small entrepreneurs, and by the fact that the frontier remained open to those who wished to enter farming.[15]

A person's status was usually closely related to the property he could obtain and to the improvements he could make upon it by his own efforts. Frequently there was a rather clear connection between his individual ability, initiative, persistence, and thrift on the one hand, and his economic success and his status on the other hand. This was true not only because of economic conditions but also because community life, where nearly everyone could be personally acquainted with nearly everyone else, was not unusual. Personal qualities not only of initiative and effort but also of honesty and sobriety could be known and appreciated and could win respect and status. Even in modern small towns status is based largely upon personal qualities of honesty, thrift, and dedicated hard work, which in the small town can be known personally apart from the objective symbols of success, such as possessions and occupational position.[16]

In the more complex society created by industrialization, a far greater variety of occupational roles than had existed heretofore came into existence, and with them a greater range of status gradations. As a few successful businessmen made great fortune, the gap between those at the top of the status system and those at the bottom widened dramatically, and between them several additional, distinguishable status groups emerged.[17] While the various classes in American society tend to spread out along a continuum without any clear dividing lines, the differences between those at some distance from each other are unmistakable. Their styles of life are quite different, and they are segregated in virtually every area of life. The sharp increase in class differences could hardly fail to increase preoccupation with status.

Status in the Bureaucratic Organization

Probably even more effective in producing an increased preoccupation with status than the increase in status differences has been the fact that industrialization and bureaucratization have led to capricious shifts in the bases for status, and thus to heightened anxiety about status. Industrialization and bureaucratization have gone hand in hand. More and more Americans carry on their daily work within great bureaucratic organizations. The once-prevalent independent entrepreneur has all but disappeared. Those who are "self-employed" now make up less than 15 percent of the working population in the United States. The rest are employees—wage workers making up more than 55 percent and salaried workers more than 30 percent of the total work force.[18] At least half of these employees work for great bureaucratic organizations—primarily government at all levels, including the military, and the largest private businesses.[19] With the constant introduction of technological improvements which tend to lead toward minuter divisions of labor, a need arises for more elaborate organization in order to coordinate the minutely divided tasks. Thus industrialization and bureaucratization accompany each other. Since both developments constantly bring new divisions of labor, they constantly undermine existing status systems.

By increasing divisions of labor, the managers of bureaucratic organizations not only achieve greater efficiency for the organization but they also reduce the need for skilled workers and render their employees more easily replaceable. The employees' status and security are undermined, and they are made more dependent upon the employer.[20] Hence anxiety about status increases. The development of skills and the replacement of skills occurs repeatedly in modern industry. When a worker spends long years in developing a skill, his status rises as his skill develops. After he has mastered his job, his status is well assured as long as his skill remains scarce and needed. But machinery requiring only unskilled attendants repeatedly replaces skilled workers, destroying their sources of status along with their jobs.[21]

As the capriciously shifting bases for status heighten preoccupation with status, this preoccupation is employed by management to further organizational goals, and thus becomes all the more deeply entrenched. Status differences in the bureaucracy usually correlate with differences in authority. These differences are useful partly in order to ensure that commands will be accepted as binding when they are communicated down the bureaucratic hierarchy of authority and status.[22] But also, status differences can be used as incentives to cooperation.[23] Mills puts it as follows: "When many small gradations in status exist, the employee can more often experience the illusion of 'being somebody' and of ascending the scale."[24] Not only management but also the unions contribute to this emphasis on status. Unions usually resist changes in traditional evaluations of status and often insist that differences in skill be recognized in differential wage rates.[25] Management failure to recognize even slight differences in the skills demanded by different jobs can lead to serious grievances among workers.[26]

Wage workers generally have the lowest status in the bureaucracy and are most alienated from those who control the organization. They have experienced earlier and longer than other groups the status insecurities created by technological innovations and have borne the brunt of economic recessions. With minute division of labor, many wage workers perform tasks far beneath their ability, and can harbor little realistic hope that their real ability will be recognized. They tend to assert their claims for income and status by open opposition to management through labor unions. As the unions have succeeded in overcoming some of the insecurities of their status and have gained larger shares of the national income, they have created insecurities among other groups. These in turn have been forced to organize, as many public school teachers have done, and to join in the clamor for recognition of their status claims. As numerous groups take part in the jockeying for power and prestige, preoccupation with status tends to become intensified throughout the society.

White-collar employees may well be more vulnerable to status anxieties than wage workers. They share many of the status insecurities of wage laborers—including destruction of skilled jobs by the introduction of machinery and by the division of labor, and frequently the necessity to perform routine work allowing them little opportunity to display or to gain recognition for their real abilities.[27] But most white-collar employees do not find open opposition to management through unionization congenial to their style of life. Their claims to status have rested largely upon their alleged superiority to the blue-collar wage workers, who are largely unionized. White-collar employees have gained prestige from their close relationships with management, and they tend to entertain hopes of moving into managerial ranks.[28] Unable to adopt the unions' open antagonism toward management, they must rely for their security and status in the organization primarily upon the goodwill of management. It is not surprising that they should suffer a good deal of uneasiness about their status.

Few people enter the ranks of management without a willingness to join in the ongoing competition for higher-status positions. Although a great deal of experience and skill may be required for the performance of managerial roles, clear, objective criteria for achievement are often lacking or are in themselves insufficient criteria for judging status. Rather, the individual is judged largely by his superiors' reactions—which are seldom revealed to him clearly and unambiguously. Possibilities for self-deception about his standing are limitless. Sometimes the executive has little idea why he advances or not and little idea precisely who in the organization is responsible for his status.[29] The rising executive must be careful not only to make correct policy decisions but also to impress their merits upon superiors tactfully so that he gains their support.[30] The managerial environment, where status is based largely on subjective judgments, encourages concern, if not anxiety, about status.

In an earlier entrepreneurial society, status grew in a rather direct way from a person's ability, initiative, and effort. In contemporary bureaucratic society, however, an individual cannot be so certain that his own ability, initiative, and effort will bring rewards in status. He is told that he ought to exercise initiative and effort, but he is often too much at the mercy of impersonal economic forces and often relies too much on capricious judgments made by others to be sure that his effort will pay off in status. Unable to enjoy confidence in status gained by his own consistent effort, and forced into manipulating other people, he is driven toward considerable preoccupation with status.

Symbols of Status

A major symptom of the preoccupation with status in the United States is the great emphasis on outward and visible symbols which proclaim status. Concern about symbols of status pervades both the bureaucratic work situation and the wider society. The white-collar and the managerial ranks in the bureaucratic organization are especially likely to be conscious of minute differences in indications of status in the office environment. The size and location of one's desk and office, the extent of one's office decorations, the washroom one is entitled to use, the people one can address by nickname, and many other details of office life are often observed very closely for indications that status is being gained, lost, or maintained.[31]

If the corporation for which a manager works is especially noted for its achievements in the business world, the manager can enjoy greater prestige than could a man of similar rank with a little-known company. Grateful for the prestige that he gains by his identification with a great corporation, the executive is usually quite willing to take its goals as his own.[32]

In our increasingly impersonal urbanized society, the status a person gains in his occupation does not readily carry over into other spheres of life where he is a stranger. Thus Americans have been impelled to demonstrate their status claims—or to assert their status pretensions—by the way in which they spend their money. Unconsciously as well as consciously, Americans constantly evaluate their fellow citizens by their expenditures for the house and its decor, for the automobile, for clothing, and for recreation. They can hardly help being aware that they themselves are being similarly evaluated.

Community studies have repeatedly revealed that the house and its location are among the most important indicators of status.[33] Apparently in the suburb, housing can be an especially sensitive index of status. Whyte found that men's promotions on the job and their families' moves to better suburban housing were closely correlated. Park Forest, a community inhabited largely by families of junior executives to whom promotions tended to come rather quickly almost as a matter of course, had an annual turnover of 35 percent in its rental apartments and 20 percent in its homes.[34]

Since good clothing is accessible through mass production to most income levels, status is revealed in subtle differences, thus encouraging a high degree of sensitivity to the differences.[35] Automobiles, however, are easily differentiated. They can be prized symbols of status to workers who lack opportunities to earn status through the full use of their abilities. Others with frustrated status aspirations can gain occasional, brief, glorious gratification through lavishly expensive weekends or vacations.[36]

Since the beginning of the present century, consumer expenditures in the United States, as indicated in the last chapter, have grown enormously. Consumers' appetites continue to be whetted by the growing number and variety of items available to them, by unceasing advertising, and by the availability of credit which makes large purchases possible without savings. There can be little question that the increased emphasis on consumption is both an expression of Americans' preoccupation with status and a factor contributing to that preoccupation.

The "American Dream"

Conscious preoccupation with status is promoted by an ideology that pervades American culture—the ideology of success, sometimes called the "American Dream." Its message is so well known that it needs little emphasis here. The Dream is symbolized by the name of Horatio Alger, in whose memory an award is given annually with formal ceremonies to some American who has risen from humble origins to great achievement.[37] It promises Americans that hard work, thrift, diligence, honesty, sobriety, and readiness to seize opportunities, along with shrewd use of one's native wit can and do lead to high achievement in the world of occupation with rich rewards in wealth and in status. This ideology is thought to be especially characteristic of the latter half of the nineteenth century when industrialization was in its boisterous youth. But it continues to be propagated constantly in the mass media, in fiction, in the churches, in the schools, and even informally through the family.[38]

To be sure, the widespread publicity which is given to the American Dream does not assure its universal acceptance. The lower social classes generally accept it less than do the middle and upper classes. This ideology, however, is a prominent part of the social environment which helps to promote preoccupation with status in the United States. How effectively does it do so? A precise answer to this question is not available. But in a poll taken in 1945, nearly 90 percent of a sampling of both "middle class" and "working class" people from all over the United States expressed confidence that their children had "just as good a chance, or a better chance to rise in the world as anybody else's."[39] About 68 percent of the same sample said they had a good chance to get ahead in their present line of work.[40] Even the great depression of the 1930's had failed to cause any extensive disillusionment with the American Dream of opportunity for all.[41]

Social Mobility: Reality and Belief

It is widely agreed among students of social stratification that at the present time in American society enough upward social mobility exists to render the American Dream quite credible. After having carefully considered the evidence available from many studies, Kahl concludes that there is considerable mobility.

> Between one half and three quarters of the men who are in professional, business, clerical, or skilled jobs have climbed relative to their fathers. No wonder they feel that our society is open, for . . . they find that most of their colleagues have moved up in the occupational (and thus the class) hierarchy.
> . . . The amount of mobility that has occurred has been multiplied by the fact that most sons who move do so by only one or two steps in the hierarchy; thus one new job at the top may make it possible for two or three sons to have an advance.[42]

To be sure, the American Dream of success in its most radical form—the "rags to riches" myth—is rarely realized in fact. But dramatic rises in status occur sufficiently often, and gain sufficient publicity when they do, that the myth constantly gains renewed vitality. Furthermore, since a majority of Americans have firsthand experience with at least slight upward mobility, their faith in the ideology of success is constantly verified and their preoccupation with status is constantly reinforced. Social scientists seem to be in general agreement that there is a great deal of social mobility in the United States.[43]

In recent years, though, some scholars have suggested that

opportunities for upward social mobility have been decreasing.[44] The evidence for this claim is inconclusive.[45] Nevertheless, it appears that some Americans are worried that opportunities to raise their status are decreasing, or that upward mobility is becoming more difficult. Such anxiety expresses an increased concern about status. Indeed, the very fact that social scientists have in the last generation or so become intensely interested in the whole area of social stratification—not to mention their concern whether mobility is declining—is probably symptomatic of a generally increasing preoccupation with status.

Emphasis on Status in the Educational System

The sector of American life where clearest evidence for increasing concern with status can be seen is that of education. Our occupational system at present is demanding more and more highly trained people, not only at the upper levels, but at all levels. Increasingly, the college degree is becoming a minimum requirement for entry into the higher-prestige occupations, and "education has become the most frequently used means for social advancement in the class system."[46] It is becoming necessary for increasing numbers of children to go farther with their education than their parents did in order to maintain a social standing equal to that of their parents.[47] The pressure to achieve success in school has been building up from a level already rather high.

The training that children in the United States receive in the public schools is designed primarily as preparation for the world of occupation. Not only do the schools provide training for various forms of work, but they also introduce children to the system of rewards that prevails in the adult world, with especial emphasis on the reward of status, and attempt to motivate them to seek these rewards through their achievements. A primary instrument by which the schools initiate pupils into the system of rewards prevailing in the adult world is the grading system. Throughout their school careers, the students' achievements are constantly being evaluated by means of examinations and ranked high or low by means of grades.

Largely on the basis of grades achieved even as early as the elementary years, the schools sort out the students and direct them toward different occupational roles with different statuses. Some are moved into college-preparatory work and others into "commercial" or "vocational" studies. Those not chosen for the college-preparatory course of study, a majority, are already cut off rather effectively from possibilities for higher education. They enter the work force upon graduation from high school, if not earlier, and take the less prestigious jobs—skilled, unskilled, clerical, sales, and the like. Differentiation of status continues in the colleges. Some students through high academic achievement are enabled to move toward graduate study and the professions.[48] Thus the educational system promotes the sort of preoccupation with status that the occupational system in the United States requires.

With an awareness of the standing conferred by the grading system and its far-reaching effects upon status in the adult world, many students become intensely concerned with their status. Parents' anxieties about the regular "report card"— satirized in scores of cartoons every year—heighten the students' consciousness of the status that they are achieving or failing to achieve. At present, these anxieties of both students and parents, which are fostered by the very structure of the school system, seem to be increasing.

These heightening anxieties over educational achievement and status tend to focus upon the problem of getting into college. Not only is a growing proportion of young people attending college but also the 1960's have seen a population explosion at the college level. The overcrowding of the colleges and universities has been keenly and even painfully felt among many families with teen-agers making application to college. This increased preoccupation with status that is presently associated with the increased demand for education may be a temporary phenomenon. Yet with the increasingly crucial role that education has been playing in the business of gaining status, the educational system is likely to remain a vital factor in promoting preoccupation with status in the United States.

Youth Culture

A symptom of the great and growing concern with status in our educational system can be seen in our youth culture. Over against the value of academic achievement in preparation for the world of occupation, our youth culture places the values of athletics and glamour. A recent study of ten high schools revealed that the majority of the boys preferred to be remembered as star athletes rather than brilliant students, and the majority of the girls preferred to be remembered as most popular or as leaders in extracurricular activities. Leading crowds among both boys and girls represent the youth-culture values rather than academic values.[49] Moreover, the schools officially reinforce the emphasis on athletics and glamour by sponsoring elaborate programs of interscholastic athletics, with cheerleaders, marching bands, and drum majorettes. The emphasis on these values appears to be increasing among teen-agers,[50] and seems to be reaching even preteens, as with Little League baseball.

The intensity and pervasiveness of youth culture is probably an indication of the great preoccupation with status in American society. Enjoyment of the status which one can achieve in the world of occupation must often be postponed until some time in the distant and dubious future. Meanwhile, as the schools begin singling out some for success and others for failure, great pressure is placed upon the teen-age students to show some signs of success. It becomes clear to the student that the status he has inherited from his parents is being withdrawn and that he must achieve his own status by his own effort. The threat of failure can loom large, and the need for immediate assurances of success can become urgent. Through athletics or glamour, one can achieve immediate success with much less effort than is required for academic and occupational success. There is the further possibility, though usually remote, that such success might be parlayed into a full-time job. Perhaps adults encourage youth culture partly because they want immediate success for their children and partly because they can identify vicariously with the success of athletes and entertainers. While youth culture upholds values that are ostensibly different from the basic values of our educational and occupational systems, it reaffirms and reinforces the allegiance paid by these systems to the achievement of success, and to preoccupation with status.

Class Differences in Striving for Status

Scanty but consistent evidence indicates that people of the higher social classes are much more likely to believe in the success values of American culture and in their own opportunities for success, and are much more likely to be striving for success and to be willing to postpone immediate gratification in order to improve their status, than are people of the lower social classes. This appears to be not merely an accommodation to available opportunities but a level of aspiration that is internalized at an age too early for a realistic evaluation of opportunity to have been made.[51] People of the lower social classes are not only less likely to enter the competitive struggle to improve their status, but also they are likely to be especially concerned about security in their jobs.[52] Neither pattern is conducive to social action.

Those who are interested primarily in security in their jobs either have been undergoing a process of socialization on the job which rather effectively destroys the sort of initiative that is essential for social action, or else demonstrate that they al-

ready lacked such initiative when they took their jobs. Those
who have sufficient initiative, drive, and resourcefulness for social action are the very people who are likely to have the abilities necessary for success in the existing order. It is not easy
for them to resist the enticements of high income and status
which are available for competent performance in the occupational roles that play key parts in supporting the existing order.

The various social classes also behave quite differently, as
we have seen in Chapter 5, in their degree of participation in
voluntary associations. Both membership and leadership in voluntary associations are concentrated among people of the
higher classes. This is, incidentally, a rather curious fact, since
men of the higher classes are more likely to hold jobs that demand a good deal of time and energy outside regular working
hours. People of the lower classes participate in voluntary associations less even though they have more time to do so. I have
accounted for the class difference in voluntary participation
by indicating that lower-class people who have the initiative
and leadership talent necessary for social action tend to be
drained off into the higher social classes. As a consequence,
those with sufficient initiative to work for social change are
seldom interested in doing so because they tend to be satisfied
with the existing order in which they enjoy, or expect to enjoy,
enviable privileges. Those whose dissatisfaction might be a
useful stimulus to social action are generally too untrained and
too discouraged to take the necessary initiative. Thus social
action, left to voluntary initiative, is left with very little impetus.

There are additional reasons for the class differences in voluntary participation. People of the higher classes participate in
key voluntary associations partly to ensure their influence—if
not control—over community affairs.[53] And—more important
for our present purpose—people of all classes participate in
voluntary associations in order to maintain, to confirm, or to
improve their status. But higher-class people participate more
partly because they are more likely to be oriented toward the

success values of American culture, partly because they have better chances for remaining mobile during larger proportions of their careers, and partly because more types of voluntary participation are likely to help them in their careers than is the case with lower-class people. Thus the preoccupation with status that is stimulated primarily in the occupational sector of the social system, and that seriously obstructs motivation for social action there, spills over into the area of voluntary participation to obstruct social action there too.

One can, of course, expect people to participate in business and professional associations and in labor unions out of concern for their status. But they also join other types of associations in order to improve their status. Among these are health and welfare organizations like the National Foundation for Infantile Paralysis. According to the study directed by Sills, 22 percent of the Foundation's volunteers said that they joined in order to advance their status. Another 23 percent said they were fulfilling job obligations—which I would take to mean maintaining or improving their occupational status. As Sills indicates, some felt that working with the Foundation was a burdensome but necessary adjunct to their jobs, whereas others, such as young, unestablished lawyers and insurance men, were attempting to make business contacts. The remaining 55 percent claimed to have joined in order to fulfill obligations to the community, to help others, or to eliminate polio.[54] It is not impossible that some of this 55 percent were also motivated by status concerns that they preferred not to mention or of which they were unconscious.

A mass of evidence has been accumulated to support the conclusion that class position has extensive influence on values and on behavior in every area of life. People of widely different social classes differ markedly at many points.[55] Their differences in behavior reflect different styles of life, leading to segregation among classes. People of sharply differing classes seldom have close personal contact with one another. Hollingshead's study of social stratification among youth in a Midwest-

ern town, having identified five social classes, showed clearly
that high school students maintained little friendship or courtship across class lines, and where crossing of class lines took
place, it seldom went farther than the nearest class.[56] Social
segregation indicates a serious problem of alienation among
the various classes. This alienation, generally regarded as normal and natural and often justified as right and proper, seems
to be accepted with indifference by most people in the United
States. The ties of human concern and sympathy which are essential elements in motivation for social action are thus all too
tenuous.

Concern for Income and Status vs. Concern for Social Action

This chapter and the preceding one have focused attention
upon the very effective system of social control which provides
powerful support for the existing order in the United States by
ensuring loyal performance in the world of occupation. If this
system of social control employed primarily negative sanctions,
it would probably not be nearly so effective as it is. That is, if
it emphasized loss of income and status for failure to hold
some job without considerable rewards in income and status
for loyal performance in the job, it would probably arouse a
good deal of resentment and opposition rather than support.
But as it is, striving for these rewards, which are rather widely
available, becomes a consuming preoccupation with a great
many Americans.

For those who hold the more rewarding occupational positions, working at the job need not be thought of primarily as
an obligation. It can be regarded as an opportunity to gain
enticing rewards. Beyond a certain level of success in many of
the more rewarding occupations, access to still greater rewards
becomes increasingly easy. Those who are able to gain the rewards and who find them enticing are not likely to be suffi-

ciently critical of the existing order to be interested in social action. Those who are able to gain the rewards, but who do not find them enticing because they are critical of the existing order, are less likely to seek the more influential occupational roles that might offer opportunities for social action.

To summarize, there are at least three major ways by which our occupational system, along with its system of social control, erects obstacles against social action through the job: (1) In the pivotal bureaucratic organizations which dominate the occupational world, the realities of power—mentioned above, but not analyzed in detail—discourage social action. That is, the centralization of power in the bureaucracy leaves those at the lower levels with little influence for social action, and the inflexibility of bureaucratic goals leaves those at the upper levels little freedom to introduce social action. (2) The income and status that are gained through the job are so essential to most Americans that they seldom even consider engaging in social action with its attendant risks to the job. (3) So enticing are the rewards of income and status provided through the job that they induce an uncritical attitude toward the existing order which offers the rewards, and this attitude carries beyond the job into voluntary participation.

9

Can the Social Pressures Against Social Action Be Overcome?

SOCIAL ACTION is urgently needed. Rapid changes taking place within the United States and around the world are constantly creating new social problems of appalling magnitude, many of which endanger the very survival of the human race. There is desperate need on every hand for vigorous activity on behalf of justice and reconciliation. What hope is there that concerned individual Americans can provide some of the needed impulse toward social action?

Judging by the thesis presented in these pages, and by the evidence marshaled to support it, there appears to be little hope. Since social action is left almost entirely to voluntary initiative while job and family obligations monopolize the bulk of the individual's time and energies, little leisure is left for social action and, probably more important, little incentive is available to arouse commitment to it. The major incentives available in American society are concentrated upon ensuring commitment to faithful performance of job and family roles, which provide rather uncritical support for the existing social order. Connected especially with the job are incentives, primarily in the form of rewards in status and in income, which not only obstruct impulses toward social action in the job but also create interests that obstruct motivation for social action outside the job. Since the instruments of social control in American society so heavily favor the existing order and obstruct motivation for social action in so many ways, what hope can there be for initiative in social action?

The thesis argued in these pages was so formulated that it evoked little evidence but that which presented the case against possibilities for a vital impulse toward social action. But an important qualification, already mentioned, must be stressed again. American society does at some points encourage social action.

Social Support for Needed Social Action

The United States enjoys an enormous advantage over the totalitarian regime that ruthlessly crushes opposition. The sort of opposition to the existing order that is necessary for social action in the United States is not forbidden. On the contrary, it is officially sanctioned. Americans are legally free to take initiative in social action. Although the dominant cultural values subtly but powerfully obstruct social action, the American social system, nevertheless, at the same time encourages it by providing channels through which needed social change can be introduced. Thus, opportunities to engage in social action are always available.

To be sure, this does not mean that social action can be expected to be easy. Complex power structures and established interests—in American communities, in large-scale voluntary associations, and in governmental, business, and other bureaucracies—provide abundant difficulties. If one is not unduly sanguine about the extent of change he intends to accomplish, however, he can expect through arduous, long-term, persistent effort, in cooperation with others, to make some significant contribution to needed social change.

Moreover, certain elements of the power situation can be turned to advantage. With the routine exercise of power concentrated in the hands of relatively few, a few people dedicated to social action can discover who wields power relevant to the problem at hand, and can learn to exert pressure and influence for needed change far out of proportion to their numbers. Those who occupy key positions of power seem to be sensitive to persistent pressure—a matter that Jesus noted when he spoke of the widow who kept pestering the unrighteous judge until she wore him down and gained vindication (Luke 18:1–8). Thus those who have concern for justice and reconciliation in the social order need not be intimidated by the structures of entrenched power and interest.

It is encouraging that in American society opportunities for achieving significant contributions in social action abound. Ordinarily missing, however, and vitally needed are initiative, leadership, and commitment to social action which will actually take advantage of the opportunities available. These appear to be the most difficult assets to obtain for the enterprise of social action. American society offers some encouragement at this point too.

Almost universally acknowledged in the United States are the ideals of democracy which favor justice for all, and which favor the view that citizens have responsibility to work actively for needed social change. Furthermore, culturally approved religious ideals which demand radical, self-giving love in human relationships are freely and widely taught. To be sure, where injustices exist, these values are ordinarily rendered innocuous because they are honored more in theory than in practice. But they are not nullified. The possibility of taking them seriously remains. Thus, most movements for social action evoke not only opposition but also a good deal of favorable sentiment, and sometimes a good deal of active support. There is a culturally approved liberalism in the United States that is sensitive to injustices and that takes seriously the responsibility to correct them.[1] The ideal of social responsibility is sufficiently potent in American society that it sometimes helps individuals to overcome the social resistance to social action.

Need for Occupations in Social Action

A major contention of these pages has been that American society works against itself by relegating social action to the status of voluntary, leisure-time activity. Building upon the support for social action that already exists in American society, however, steps could be taken and are already being taken here and there to remedy in some degree this defect in our social system. It should be possible in our affluent society to establish more and more full-time occupational roles that are specifically devoted toward initiating social action in various specialized areas. Money for such purposes would, of course, be difficult to acquire, but might be obtained through bequests and foundation grants. Although the foundations are generally aligned with the existing order, they can transcend the immediate present and can seek the long-term well-being of the community. The initiative for establishing such occupational positions must come, of course, from intense voluntary effort!

Moreover, certain already existing occupational roles might be modified to include social action in increasing proportions. Already some elements of the social work profession have been moving in this direction. The executive ranks in the corporations might give increasing consideration to possibilities for employing corporate power in social action. They might hire consultants or staff of their own to advise them on the long-range social impact of corporate activities, and to seek imaginatively for specific steps in social action that particular companies might take. Many who are teaching in colleges and universities have interests that impinge on social action. They might create interdepartmental programs to analyze social problems in depth, and to explore approaches to social action both through voluntary associations and through various occupations. Such programs might include opportunities for deliberation on crucial issues, not only among students and faculty of various disciplines, but also among people active in business, in government, and in the professions. In short, much might be done to institutionalize impulses toward social action in American society by creating occupational roles committed to social action. But such roles can be created only through voluntary initiative!

Voluntary Initiative in Social Action

The need for voluntary initiative in social action might be reduced in American society, but it is most unlikely to be eliminated. In our rapidly changing society, institutions can quickly become obsolete. Even those committed to social action may need constant pressure from voluntary effort to keep them relevant. The accelerating pace of social change rapidly creates new social problems with which existing institutions are ill-equipped to cope. Thus we can expect that needed social action will remain heavily dependent upon voluntary initiative.

The tragic fact remains that social pressures against voluntary initiative in social action seldom lose their ascendancy over the lives of most Americans. To be sure, times come in the lives of everyone when the pressures are considerably less pervasive and powerful. For example, retired people and nonworking women with older children have no job obligations, and their family obligations are generally light. Hence, they might have exceptional freedom to engage in social action through voluntary associations. Or again, men around fifty years of age and older may have vested rights in their pensions, may have less debt and less urgent demands on larger income, may have achieved relatively secure status in their jobs, and may be at the height of their influence in their jobs. They might have exceptional freedom to initiate social action through their jobs. Many other cases of unusual freedom from the pressures against social action could be cited. But apparently few people recognize their intervals of freedom as opportunities for social action, probably because the societal pressures have already so effectively eliminated the option of social action from serious consideration.

Each person must judge for himself the extent to which the social pressures against social action enumerated here affect him. Perhaps it is rather depressing to contemplate how intricate and pervasive are these pressures in which some of us are deeply entangled, and from which none of us can entirely escape. But at the same time, conscious recognition of these pressures already renders them less potent. When they are spread out before us, it becomes quite apparent that they need not control us.

Let us consider the plight of the concerned person who is profoundly disturbed by the appalling social injustices that engulf us, and who sincerely longs to help in achieving some greater degree of justice in our collective life, but who feels powerless before problems that appear to be quite overwhelming. Many of us find ourselves in such a plight. Our sense of helplessness may appear to be quite reasonable before the enormous complexities of social injustices, and before the intricacies of power in our society. However, as argued above, the fact is that steady, persistent, long-term struggle can win small but significant social changes. We cannot realistically blame the complexities of injustices or the intricacies of power for our inaction. But we tend to do so, nevertheless. Our unrealistic sense of helplessness can be understood only if we take into consideration the social pressures against social action whose impact we ordinarily fail to appreciate because we are not fully conscious of them.

Recognizing how difficult it is for us to initiate social action in a society that defines such activity as merely voluntary, and that provides powerful instruments of social control to ensure that we fulfill obligations supporting the existing order, we can better understand our feeling of helplessness. But recognizing these pressures, we need not remain helpless. Indeed, recognizing them, we can only in "bad faith"[2] deny that we have freedom to initiate social action. To be sure, initiating social action may require risks and sacrifices of us. These do not excuse us, however. They do not give us license to claim insufficient freedom for social action. In freedom, we decide whether or not to take these risks or to make these sacrifices.

To initiate social action through the job ordinarily involves, as discussed above, some risk of losing the job or of losing chances for promotion. Few of us even consider taking such a risk. But let us consider it now! Let us recognize that we have freedom to decide whether we will be so dependent upon the job for regular income and for status that we will refuse to consider initiating social action through the job. We can choose which things will mean most to us. It would be unrealistic to expect that we could eliminate completely our desires for income and for status. But we can decide that they will not be sufficiently determinative in our lives to prevent us from engaging in social action.

Moreover, it would be unrealistic for us to expect that we could escape our culturally prescribed obligations to the job and to the family. We can expect these obligations to remain pressing, and we can expect social action, either through the voluntary association or through the job, with some exceptions, to remain voluntary. We can expect our time for social action to remain limited. But we need not give the same priority to job and to family obligations as our society does. We can still make social action one of our fundamental commitments, and we can carve out a large area of freedom to engage in it. At least we can decide to give nearly all our voluntary time to social action.

Only in "bad faith" can we claim that we have no voluntary time available. Many of us, however, fail to preserve our freedom even during our "free time." We allow ourselves to be pressured into all sorts of activities that are not our own and in which we have little real interest. We join the bridge club, accept an office in the P.T.A., work on the church rummage sale, raise money for the Community Chest, serve as a volunteer at the hospital, and the like, not because we really want to, but because we cannot think of good excuses for refusing. Those who are especially conscientious, and thus good candidates for social action, are especially likely to find themselves on this treadmill, resenting it, but not knowing how to escape it. In order to work in social action, however, we must eliminate or at least drastically reduce all other voluntary activities. Once involved in social action on some single, limited issue, we may become more busy than ever, but our activity can be exhilarating rather than burdensome because we use our time for creative activity of our own to meet vital human needs that might otherwise have remained unalleviated.

One can initiate social action either by joining some existing group or by starting a new one. In either case, the person's sense of vitality, excitement, and involvement in the effort will probably be roughly proportional to the extent to which he maintains independence to make his own contribution to the task at hand. This is not to say that he must gain a commanding position. On the contrary, working cooperatively with others can be far more stimulating and rewarding. He simply needs to feel that he has plenty of freedom for his own creative innovation, and that his contributions, even if they become modified by others, are vital and essential to the effort.

Probably the easiest way to fulfill these conditions is to start one's own project in social action. One need not be overwhelmed by the difficulties involved. The first step is simply to discern some intensely urgent social problem, or segment of a problem, within the scope of one's influence. The second step is to determine that one will give priority to acting on this problem, over a long period if need be. The third step is to find a few other people with whom one can establish cooperative working relationships, who see the great urgency of the same problem, and who are willing to make a similar commitment to act on it. The remaining steps need not be planned in advance. A thoroughly committed group of concerned people can discover power to act together that they could never have imagined alone. To be sure, they face all sorts of pitfalls which might frustrate their efforts and lead to disillusionment. But if they remain flexible and imaginative, and they can experience from initiating a creative movement of needed social change is hard to duplicate.

As most of the preceding pages have testified, American society, in its legitimate attempt to induce individuals to carry out tasks that make possible its day-to-day survival, obstructs realistic about their goals, they might have to change direction a good deal, but they can avert defeat. The exhilaration that social action which could make possible its long-range survival. Not only does American society thus work to its own detriment, but it also works to the detriment of individuals within it. It works not only against the stake of individuals in the long-range survival of the society but also against their need for fulfillment through creative activity which meets genuine human needs. There is no panacea either for society or for the individual. But those individuals who assert their freedom by initiating social action contribute vitally to a more stable as well as to a more just society, and at the same time open new horizons for personal fulfillment.

Notes

Notes

Chapter 1. SOCIAL ACTION:
FULFILLMENT OF TWO DIVERGENT NEEDS

1. For an extensive account of many such injustices, see Roger L. Shinn, *Tangled World* (Charles Scribner's Sons, 1965).

2. "Social action" might refer to any effort toward bringing about change of any kind in the institutions of society. But I shall mean consistently in these pages effort to bring about change in the direction of justice and reconciliation. For further clarification of this key term, see Ch. 4.

3. Just one example: Erich Fromm, *The Sane Society* (Holt, Rinehart and Winston, Inc., 1955).

4. This is a major claim, but I will not attempt to support it here since it is not essential to my basic thesis. I simply hope that my view strikes a sympathetic chord in the reader!

Chapter 2. SOCIAL PRESSURES AGAINST NEEDED SOCIAL ACTION

1. For vivid descriptions of oppression suffered in the ghetto, see William Stringfellow, *My People Is the Enemy* (Holt, Rinehart and Winston, Inc., 1964), and Malcolm X, assisted by Alex Haley, *The Autobiography of Malcolm X* (Grove Press, Inc., 1965).

2. C. Wright Mills, *White Collar: The American Middle Classes* (Oxford University Press, Inc., 1951), p. xvi.

3. Two books that provide excellent reviews and critiques of the recent studies of community power are Nelson W. Polsby, *Community Power and Political Theory* (Yale University Press, 1963), and Arnold M. Rose, *The Power Structure: Political Process in American Society* (Oxford University Press, Inc., 1967). For differing views regarding power on the national scene, see C. Wright

Mills, *The Power Elite* (Oxford University Press, Inc., 1956), and Talcott Parsons, *Structure and Process in Modern Societies* (The Free Press of Glencoe, 1960), Ch. 6.

Chapter 3. THE EXISTING ORDER

1. Hence my preference for the term "existing order" over the term *"status quo,"* since the latter tends to be associated with a static order.

2. The same claim can be safely made for any functioning social system, for the very fact that it continues to function depends upon arrangements of power to ensure its continuance. The view of power expressed here is drawn from the general perspective of sociology—especially from the structural-functionalist school—and from cultural anthropology as well. This view is expressed in the theory of social control; a good review of writings on social control is given in Don Martindale, *American Society* (D. Van Nostrand Company, Inc., 1960), Ch. 15.

3. See John Kenneth Galbraith, *The Affluent Society* (Houghton Mifflin Company, 1958), especially pp. 133 ff.

4. John Kenneth Galbraith, *American Capitalism: The Concept of Countervailing Power* (2d ed., Houghton Mifflin Company, 1956), p. 27.

5. There is much debate over whether the economic or the political factor predominates. A balanced view of the relative power of each is given by Parsons, *Structure and Process in Modern Societies*, Ch. 6.

6. When the survival of the nation is threatened, as it was especially in World War II, the requirement of loyalty to the nation, including if necessary a willingness to die in battle, takes priority over all other obligations. So wholeheartedly has this social obligation become accepted among the American people that the nation can rely largely on voluntary adherence to the norm, and need not always exercise its coercive power through the government to ensure fulfillment of the obligation. Indeed, if all peoples of the world can in any sense be said to share a common culture, it is in their common acceptance of the value of nationalism—a very dangerous situation.

7. A very clear statement of our culturally defined obligations appears in Bernard Barber, " 'Mass Apathy' and Voluntary Social Participation in the United States" (unpublished Ph.D. dissertation, Harvard University, 1948), pp. 13–19. Barber's fine dissertation has been a key influence upon the writing of the present volume. Tal-

cott Parsons frequently deals with the culturally defined obligations, but seldom uses the word "obligation," preferring "role" or "role-expectation." See, e.g., *The Social System* (The Free Press of Glencoe, 1951), pp. 185–186, 236–243; *Structure and Process in Modern Societies*, pp. 229, 340; Talcott Parsons and Robert F. Bales, *Family Socialization and Interaction Process* (The Free Press of Glencoe, 1955), pp. 13, 124, 129. The priority of the job is discussed thoroughly in Robert S. and Helen Merrell Lynd, *Middletown: A Study in Contemporary American Culture* (Harcourt, Brace & Company, Inc., 1929), Chs. 4 to 7.

8. Robert S. and Helen Merrell Lynd, *Middletown in Transition: A Study in Cultural Conflicts* (Harcourt, Brace & Company, Inc., 1937), p. 7.

9. Hsiao-Tung Fei, "Peasantry and Gentry: An Interpretation of Chinese Social Structure and Its Changes," *American Journal of Sociology*, Vol. 52 (July, 1946), pp. 1–17.

10. Stuart A. Queen, Robert W. Habenstein, and John B. Adams, *The Family in Various Cultures* (J. B. Lippincott Company, 1961), pp. 138–158.

11. Talcott Parsons, "The Kinship System of the Contemporary United States," *The American Anthropologist*, Vol. 45 (January, 1943), pp. 23–28; Robin M. Williams, Jr., *American Society: A Sociological Interpretation* (2d ed., Alfred A. Knopf, Inc., 1960), pp. 50–52. For exceptions to the prevailing pattern and qualifications to the prevailing view, see Marvin Sussman, "The Isolated Nuclear Family: Fact or Fiction," *Social Problems*, Vol. 6 (Spring, 1959), pp. 333–340; Eugene Litwak, "Geographic Mobility and Extended Family Cohesion," *American Sociological Review*, Vol. 25 (June, 1960), pp. 385–394; Marvin Sussman and Lee Burchinal, "Kin Family Network: Unheralded Structure in Current Conceptualizations of Family Functioning," *Marriage and Family Living*, Vol. 24 (August, 1962), pp. 231–240.

12. Roy W. Fairchild and John Charles Wynn, *Families in the Church: A Protestant Survey* (Association Press, 1961), pp. 23–24.

13. Mills, *White Collar*, Chs. 6, 7.

14. Fairchild and Wynn, *op. cit.*, p. 124; John R. Seeley, R. Alexander Sim, and Elizabeth W. Loosley, *Crestwood Heights: A Study of the Culture of Suburban Life* (Basic Books, Inc., Publishers, 1956), pp. 118–120.

15. It seems unlikely at present that Title VII of the Civil Rights Act of 1964, which went into effect on July 2, 1965, and which forbids discrimination against women in job-hiring and in job promotion, will radically change this situation.

16. Parsons and Bales, *Family Socialization and Interaction Process*, pp. 13–15.

17. Talcott Parsons, *Essays in Sociological Theory* (2d ed., The Free Press of Glencoe, 1954), pp. 79–87.

18. Parsons and Bales, *op. cit.*, pp. 126–128.

19. This emphasis upon achievement through competition also has "dysfunctional" consequences for our society and for its occupational system since many people suffer disappointment in the competition for status. See Robert K. Merton, *Social Theory and Social Structure* (rev. and enl. ed., The Free Press of Glencoe, 1957), Ch. 4, "Social Structure and Anomie."

20. Parsons and Bales, *Family Socialization and Interaction Process*, pp. 126–127; Queen, Habenstein, and Adams, *The Family in Various Cultures*, p. 304; Willard Waller, *The Family: A Dynamic Interpretation* (The Cordon Co., Inc., 1938), Ch. 8.

21. Parsons and Bales, *Family Socialization and Interaction Process*, pp. 3–8.

22. Queen, Habenstein, and Adams, *The Family in Various Cultures*, pp. 303–304.

23. Mills, *White Collar*, p. 229.

24. *Ibid.*, pp. 220–238. See also Jules Henry, *Culture Against Man* (Random House, Inc., 1963), pp. 25–32.

25. Evidence that "familism" is a primary concern in movement to the suburbs appears in Wendell Bell, "Social Choice, Life Styles, and Suburban Residence," in William M. Dobriner, ed., *The Suburban Community* (G. P. Putnam's Sons, 1958), pp. 225–247.

26. Parsons and Bales, *Family Socialization and Interaction Process*, p. 16.

27. Some evidence for this contention can be found in W. A. Anderson, "The Family and Individual Social Participation," *American Sociological Review*, Vol. 8 (August, 1943), pp. 420–424. Anderson shows that active participation in community affairs "is chiefly a family trait." If parents participate, their children usually do also.

Chapter 4. A CLOSE LOOK AT SOCIAL ACTION

1. For a bibliography that includes an extensive list of philosophical and theological literature relevant to the problem of justice, see *Economic Ethics Bibliography* (Department of Economics, South Dakota State University, 1964).

2. Bruce Morgan, *Christians, the Church, and Property: Ethics*

and the Economy in a Supra-market World (The Westminster Press, 1963), p. 57.

3. Cited by Morgan, *ibid.*, p. 55. See also pp. 54–60, 208–238, for further discussion of justice and reconciliation.

4. David L. Sills, *The Volunteers: Means and Ends in a National Organization* (The Free Press of Glencoe, 1957), pp. 42–47.

5. As Peter Drucker puts it, the corporation is "without function except as the initiator of economic and technological progress." *Concept of the Corporation* (John Day Co., Inc., 1946), p. 37.

6. See above, Ch. 3.

7. Unless of course, he gains or holds a rare job requiring him to engage in social action, or unless he manages to publish a "successful" book about his experiences!

8. See above, Ch. 3.

Chapter 5. WEAKNESS OF THE IMPULSE TOWARD SOCIAL ACTION AS REVEALED IN AN ANALYSIS OF VOLUNTARY ASSOCIATIONS

1. For the results of a study of how much time people devote to their job and family obligations, see George A. Lundberg, Mirra Komarovsky, and Alice McInerny, *Leisure: A Suburban Study* (Columbia University Press, 1934), especially Table II, p. 97. Since the length of the working week has decreased since 1934, these figures should probably be revised downward for the present day.

2. See Joseph S. Zeisel, "The Workweek in American Industry 1850–1956," and Seymour L. Wolfbein, "The Changing Length of Working Life," in Eric Larrabee and Rolf Meyersohn, eds., *Mass Leisure* (The Free Press of Glencoe, 1958), pp. 145–161.

3. Lundberg, Komarovsky, and McInerny, *Leisure: A Suburban Study*, Table III, pp. 100–101. Eating was classified as a leisure-time activity because it is usually made an occasion for conversation and for relaxation from work (p. 99). Nonleisure activities were defined as sleep, paid work, care of self, transportation to and from work, and care of household and children, pp. 94–99.

4. *Ibid.*, pp. 99–111.

5. Quoted in Williams, *American Society*, pp. 494–495.

6. Lynd and Lynd, *Middletown*, pp. 285–286.

7. Edmund de S. Brunner and J. H. Kolb, *Rural Social Trends* (McGraw-Hill Book Company, Inc., 1933), pp. 102, 243.

8. Lynd and Lynd, *Middletown*, pp. 285–286.

9. W. Lloyd Warner and Paul S. Lunt, *The Social Life of a Modern Community* (Yale University Press, 1941), p. 320. Many of these associations were rather ephemeral; 357 of the total number

made up the majority of the permanent associations of the community—approximately one for each 48 citizens.

10. *Encyclopedia of Associations*, Vol. I, *National Organizations of the United States* (4th ed., Gale Research Company, 1964). See table on p. 94.

11. *Ibid.*, p. 289.

12. *Ibid.*, p. 474.

13. Sherwood Dean Fox, "Voluntary Associations and Social Structure" (unpublished Ph.D. dissertation, Harvard University, 1952), p. 73.

14. Bernard Barber, "Participation and Mass Apathy in Associations," in Alvin W. Gouldner, ed., *Studies in Leadership: Leadership and Democratic Action* (Harper & Brothers, 1950), p. 483. These studies usually exclude church membership, but count membership in church organizations.

15. Murray Hausknecht, *The Joiners* (The Bedminster Press, 1962), pp. 15–23, 127–129.

16. Herbert Goldhamer, "Some Factors Affecting Participation in Voluntary Associations" (unpublished Ph.D. dissertation, University of Chicago, 1943), p. 19.

17. Frederick A. Bushee, "Social Organizations in a Small City," *American Journal of Sociology*, Vol. 51 (November, 1945), p. 218. Calculations of some of these percentages are my own, based on data given.

18. Sills, *The Volunteers*, pp. 38–40, 59–61.

19. Barber, "Participation and Mass Apathy in Associations," pp. 484–485.

20. Brunner and Kolb, *Rural Social Trends*, pp. 243, 262–263.

21. Bushee, "Social Organizations in a Small City," p. 221.

22. Morris Axelrod, "Urban Structure and Social Participation," *American Sociological Review*, Vol. 21 (February, 1956), pp. 13–18. The date when data were collected is not given.

23. Barber, "Participation and Mass Apathy in Associations," pp. 486–487.

24. W. Lloyd Warner, *American Life: Dream and Reality* (The University of Chicago Press, 1953), p. 193. These conclusions were originally reported in Warner and Lunt, *The Social Life of a Modern Community*, p. 329.

25. *Ibid.*, pp. 329, 332–333. Calculations of percentages are my own, based on data given. For additional evidence, see Mirra Komarovsky, "The Voluntary Associations of Urban Dwellers," *American Sociological Review*, Vol. 11 (December, 1946), pp. 686–698.

26. Hausknecht, *The Joiners,* pp. 16–17, 23–25.

27. Barber, " 'Mass Apathy' and Voluntary Social Participation in the United States," p. 71. Barber gives a thorough résumé of research data supporting these conclusions in pp. 45–80. See also Leonard Reissman, "Class, Leisure, and Social Participation," *American Sociological Review,* Vol. 19 (February, 1954), pp. 76–84. There are isolated exceptions to this rule, but not enough to change the overall pattern if a representative sample of the population is analyzed. See, e.g., Komarovsky, "The Voluntary Associations of Urban Dwellers," p. 691.

28. William G. Mather, "Income and Social Participation," *American Sociological Review,* Vol. 6 (June, 1941), pp. 380–383. In 1937, only 35 percent of the families in Franklin earned $100 or more a month.

29. *Ibid.,* p. 381.

30. *Ibid.,* pp. 381–382.

31. Reissman, "Class, Leisure, and Social Participation," pp. 79–80. Calculations of percentages are my own.

32. Warner and Lunt, *The Social Life of a Modern Community,* p. 334.

33. Gunnar Myrdal, *An American Dilemma: The Negro Problem and Modern Democracy* (Harper & Brothers, 1944), Ch. 33.

34. *Ibid.,* p. 719.

35. *Ibid.,* p. 714. See also Mills, *White Collar,* pp. 346–347.

36. A thorough and well-documented analysis of lower-class discouragement is provided by Genevieve Knupfer, "Portrait of the Underdog," *Public Opinion Quarterly,* Vol. 11 (Spring, 1947), pp. 103–114.

Chapter 6. EXISTING VOLUNTARY ASSOCIATIONS

1. Arnold M. Rose, *Theory and Method in the Social Sciences* (The University of Minnesota Press, 1954), p. 51.

2. Mills, *The Power Elite,* p. 307.

3. Rose, *Theory and Method in the Social Sciences,* pp. 56, 68.

4. Mills, *The Power Elite,* p. 307.

5. Barber, " 'Mass Apathy' and Voluntary Social Participation in the United States," p. 98.

6. Barber, "Participation and Mass Apathy in Associations," pp. 488–489.

7. *Ibid.,* pp. 485, 487.

8. See Chester I. Barnard, *The Functions of the Executive* (Harvard University Press, 1938), especially pp. 216 ff.

9. Barber, "Participation and Mass Apathy in Associations," pp. 490–499.

10. John E. Tsouderas, "Organizational Change in Terms of a Series of Selected Variables," *American Sociological Review*, Vol. 20 (April, 1955), pp. 206–210.

11. Sills, *The Volunteers*, especially pp. 37–61.

12. See *ibid.*, pp. 253–271, for a good review of comment on this issue.

13. Philip Selznick, *TVA and the Grass Roots: A Study in the Sociology of Formal Organization* (University of California Press, 1949), pp. 258–259.

14. Rose, *Theory and Method in the Social Sciences*, p. 58.

15. Sills, *The Volunteers*, p. 258.

16. *Ibid.*, pp. 262–271.

17. *Ibid.*, p. 258.

18. Fox, "Voluntary Associations and Social Structure."

19. The *Encyclopedia* itself makes no claim that it presents a representative listing, but Research Editor M. E. Brown, in a letter to me dated July 28, 1964, said in part: "I do not believe that any particular category receives undue emphasis, or that any group is necessarily weak. . . ." The fifth edition was published in December, 1967, too late to be used here.

20. For a more detailed discussion of my impressions, see my "American Cultural Values Obstructing Christian Social Action" (unpublished Th.D. dissertation, Union Theological Seminary, 1966), pp. 114–143.

21. See Peter L. Berger, *The Noise of Solemn Assemblies* (Doubleday & Company, Inc., 1961), especially pp. 17–104.

22. For a thorough discussion of the goals of business associations, see Fox, "Voluntary Associations and Social Structure," Ch. 4.

23. See Victor Gotbaum, "Revolution in the Palaces of Labor," *Renewal*, June, 1965, pp. 6–7.

24. For evidence, see my dissertation, pp. 143–148.

Chapter 7. DEPENDENCE UPON THE JOB FOR INCOME AS AN OBSTACLE TO SOCIAL ACTION

1. The characteristics of bureaucratic organization have been dealt with in a growing body of recent literature. See, e.g., Peter M. Blau, *Bureaucracy in Modern Society* (Random House, Inc., 1956); Amitai Etzioni, ed., *Complex Organizations: A Sociological Reader* (Holt, Rinehart and Winston, Inc., 1961); Robert Presthus, *The*

Organizational Society: An Analysis and a Theory (Alfred A. Knopf, Inc., 1962).

2. For descriptions of restraints on business executives, see Drucker, *Concept of the Corporation*, especially Ch. 1; Peter F. Drucker, *The Practice of Management* (Harper & Brothers, 1954), especially Chs. 2, 5. On the goals of the corporation, see John Kenneth Galbraith, *The New Industrial State* (Houghton Mifflin Company, 1967), Ch. 15.

3. "Business Sets Up Its Own 'Great Society,'" *U.S. News & World Report*, April 3, 1967, pp. 73–75.

4. Galbraith, *The New Industrial State*, especially Chs. 2 to 4.

5. *Ibid.*, Ch. 15.

6. U. S. Bureau of the Census, *U.S. Census of Population: 1960, Subject Reports, Sources and Structure of Family Income*, Final Report PC(2)–4C (U.S. Government Printing Office, 1964), p. 122. Calculations of percentages are my own.

7. *Ibid.*, pp. 122, 136. Calculations of percentages are my own.

8. *Ibid.*, p. 122.

9. *Ibid.*, p. 111. Calculations of percentages are my own.

10. Whiting Williams, *Mainsprings of Men* (Charles Scribner's Sons, 1925), pp. 17–30.

11. Average family personal income per consumer unit in the United States was, in constant (1950) dollars, $3,363 in 1929 and $5,304 in 1957, according to U.S. Bureau of the Census, *Historical Statistics of the United States, Colonial Times to 1957* (U.S. Government Printing Office, 1960), p. 166, Series G–121.

12. Lynd and Lynd, *Middletown*, p. 83.

13. Lynd and Lynd, *Middletown in Transition*, pp. 10–11, 573.

14. Galbraith, *The Affluent Society*, pp. 171–172. Figures are in constant 1947 dollars.

15. In calculating these percentages I have included "personal taxes" and also "indirect business taxes"—consisting primarily of sales and excise taxes and property taxes—but not corporate profits taxes. For 1929, see U.S. Department of Commerce, Office of Business Economics, *National Income, 1954 Edition* (U.S. Government Printing Office, 1954), pp. 164, 170. For 1966, see *Survey of Current Business*, July, 1967, pp. 7–8.

16. William H. Whyte, Jr., *The Organization Man* (Anchor Books, Doubleday & Company, Inc., 1957), pp. 338–341.

17. C. Northcote Parkinson, *The Law and the Profits* (Houghton Mifflin Company, 1960), p. 5.

18. Whyte, *The Organization Man*, pp. 354–361.

19. *Ibid.*, p. 355.

20. U.S. Congress, Joint Economic Committee, *1967 Supplement to Economic Indicators* (U.S. Government Printing Office, 1967), pp. 15, 117. Calculations of percentages are my own.

21. *1962 Supplement to Economic Indicators*, p. 108. The figure may not be reliable since in subsequent issues of the *Supplement* it is listed as "not available." Calculation of percentage is my own.

22. *1967 Supplement to Economic Indicators*, p. 117. Calculation of percentage is my own.

23. George Katona *et al., 1963 Survey of Consumer Finances* (Survey Research Center, University of Michigan, 1964), p. 65; George Katona *et al., 1966 Survey of Consumer Finances* (Survey Research Center, University of Michigan, 1967), p. 33.

24. *Ibid.,* pp. 40–42, 52.

25. *1967 Supplement to Economic Indicators*, pp. 15, 117. Calculations of percentages are my own.

26. *Economic Indicators*, August, 1967, pp. 5, 32. Calculations of percentages are my own.

27. *1967 Supplement to Economic Indicators*, pp. 15, 117. Calculations of percentages are my own.

28. Information obtained upon request from National Income Division, Office of Business Economics, U.S. Department of Commerce, Washington, D.C.

29. Katona, *1966 Survey of Consumer Finances*, p. 55.

30. Insufficient data are available for the exact figure. For the basis of my estimate, see my dissertation, p. 180n.

31. Katona, *1966 Survey of Consumer Finances*, p. 65.

32. The proportion of nonfarm housing units that was owner occupied rose from 41.1 percent in 1940 to 61.0 percent in 1960. The proportion of these housing units that carried mortgage debt rose from 45.3 percent in 1940 to 56.8 percent in 1960. From U.S. Bureau of the Census, *Statistical Abstract of the United States: 1965* (U.S. Government Printing Office, 1965), pp. 758, 765. I assume that housing units correspond roughly with spending units. In 1940 mortgage debt outstanding was 23.0 percent of disposable personal income, about the same as in 1929, and in 1960 it was 40.4 percent.

33. Albert T. Sommers and Shirley Hoffman Rhine, *The New Dimension in Mortgage Debt*, Technical Paper Number 15 (National Industrial Conference Board, Inc., 1964), p. 7.

34. *Ibid.,* pp. 13–14.

35. *Ibid.,* p. 10.

36. Raymond W. Goldsmith, *A Study of Saving in the United States* (Princeton University Press, 1955), Vol. I, p. 7.

37. *1967 Supplement to Economic Indicators,* p. 15.

38. Goldsmith, *op. cit.,* p. 159. See also all of Ch. 6.

39. Pao Lun Cheng, "Consumption of Nondurable Goods and Contractual Commitment of Disposable Income," *The Review of Economics and Statistics,* Vol. 45 (August, 1963), pp. 254–255.

40. *Statistical Abstract of the United States: 1967,* p. 296.

41. *Ibid.*

42. Robert E. Dallos, "Pension Funds: Congress to Study Tighter Regulations," *The New York Times,* November 28, 1966, p. 63.

43. *Ibid.;* Bankers Trust Company, *1965 Study of Industrial Retirement Plans* (New York, 1960), pp. 19–20.

44. John I. Saks, "Status in the Labor Market," *Monthly Labor Review,* Vol. 80 (January, 1957), p. 21.

45. Bankers Trust Company, *op. cit.,* pp. 19–20; George H. Foote and David J. McLaughlin, "The President's Stake in Pension Planning," *Harvard Business Review,* Vol. 43 (September–October, 1965), pp. 91–106.

Chapter 8. DEPENDENCE UPON THE JOB FOR STATUS AS AN OBSTACLE TO SOCIAL ACTION

1. Jerry Gerasimo, "A Comparison of Social Behavior in Occupationally Mobile and Occupationally Stable Young Adults" (unpublished Ph.D. dissertation, University of Chicago, 1965), especially Ch. 5.

2. Peter M. Blau, "Social Mobility and Interpersonal Relations," *American Sociological Review,* Vol. 21 (June, 1956), pp. 290–295.

3. See, e.g., W. Lloyd Warner, with Marchia Meeker and Kenneth Eells, *Social Class in America* (Harper & Brothers, 1960).

4. Leonard Reissman, *Class in American Society* (The Free Press of Glencoe, 1959), p. 144. See also p. 361.

5. Williams, *American Society,* pp. 98–100.

6. Bernard Barber, *Social Stratification* (Harcourt, Brace and Company, 1957), pp. 307–317, 359–361; Reissman, *Class in American Society,* pp. 356–366.

7. Parsons, *Structure and Process in Modern Societies,* pp. 111–115, 147–149, 229–230.

8. Kingsley Davis, *Human Society* (The Macmillan Company, 1949), pp. 366–370; Barber, *Social Stratification,* pp. 20–30; Joseph Kahl, *The American Class Structure* (Rinehart & Company, Inc., 1957), pp. 14–18.

9. Reinhold Niebuhr, *Moral Man and Immoral Society* (Charles Scribner's Sons, 1932), p. 8.

10. Warner's study of ethnic groups reveals that, in the United States, even some of the most powerful subgroups—those with their own separate languages—have great difficulty in maintaining separate identity. American culture has been remarkably successful in drawing the members of ethnic subsystems into the mainstream of American life. The children of immigrants often try to be "more American than Americans." Although some immigrants struggle to maintain their ethnic identity, "generally speaking, our class order disunites ethnic groups and accelerates their assimilation." W. Lloyd Warner and Leo Srole, *The Social Systems of American Ethnic Groups* (Yale University Press, 1945), p. 284.

11. Lynd and Lynd, *Middletown*, p. 25; Parsons and Bales, *Family Socialization and Interaction Process*, pp. 12–13.

12. E. Wight Bakke, *Citizens Without Work* (Yale University Press, 1940).

13. Mills, *White Collar*, p. 7.

14. Kurt Mayer, "Recent Changes in the Class Structure of the United States," in Alvin W. and Helen P. Gouldner, eds., *Modern Sociology* (Harcourt, Brace and World, Inc., 1963), pp. 251–255.

15. Mills, *White Collar*, Ch. 1; Reissman, *Class in American Society*, pp. 15–16.

16. Arthur J. Vidich and Joseph Bensman, *Small Town in Mass Society* (Anchor Books, Doubleday & Company, Inc., 1960), pp. 49–51.

17. For a vivid instance of this process, see Liston Pope, *Millhands and Preachers: A Study of Gastonia* (Yale University Press, 1942), pp. viii, 5–6, 49–69.

18. Mayer, *loc. cit.*, pp. 253–254.

19. Robert Presthus, *The Organizational Society*, pp. 79–80. Presthus does not define precisely what he means by "big organization," by indicating, for example, the minimum number of employees necessary to make an organization big. But among industrial corporations he includes only the 500 largest.

20. Alvin W. Gouldner, "Metaphysical Pathos and the Theory of Bureaucracy," in Etzioni, ed., *Complex Organizations*, pp. 77–78.

21. For examples of this process, see W. Lloyd Warner and J. O. Low, *The Social System of the Modern Factory* (Yale University Press, 1947), Ch. 5; Lynd and Lynd, *Middletown*, pp. 39–44; Mills, *White Collar*, pp. 226–227, 244–245.

22. Chester I. Barnard, "Functions and Pathology of Status Systems in Formal Organizations," in William Foote Whyte, ed., *Industry and Society* (McGraw-Hill Book Company, Inc., 1946), pp. 64–68.

23. *Ibid.*, pp. 68–69.

24. Mills, *White Collar*, p. 211.

25. Jack Barbash, *The Practice of Unionism* (Harper & Brothers, 1956), pp. 124–126.

26. George C. Homans, "Status Disparity Among Clerical Workers," in Gouldner and Gouldner, eds., *Modern Sociology*, pp. 230–236.

27. Mills, *White Collar*, Ch. 9, pp. 224–228.

28. *Ibid.*, pp. 209–211, 304–314.

29. Presthus, *The Organizational Society*, pp. 144–162.

30. David Riesman, with Nathan Glazer and Reuel Denny, *The Lonely Crowd* (Anchor Books, Doubleday & Company, Inc., 1950), p. 154.

31. William H. Whyte, Jr., and the Editors of *Fortune*, *Is Anybody Listening?* (Simon and Schuster, Inc., 1952), pp. 116–119.

32. Galbraith, *The New Industrial State*, p. 154.

33. See, e.g., Seeley, Sim, and Loosley, *Crestwood Heights*, Ch. 3; A. C. Spectorsky, *The Exurbanites* (J. B. Lippincott Company, 1955).

34. Whyte, *The Organization Man*, pp. 174–175, 335.

35. Bernard Barber and Lyle S. Lobel, " 'Fashion' in Women's Clothes and the American Social System," in Reinhard Bendix and Seymour Martin Lipset, eds., *Class, Status, and Power: A Reader in Social Stratification* (The Free Press of Glencoe, 1953), pp. 323–332.

36. Mills, *White Collar*, pp. 255–258.

37. R. Richard Wohl, "The 'Rags to Riches Story': An Episode of Secular Idealism," in Bendix and Lipset, eds., *Class, Status, and Power*, p. 388.

38. See Merton, *Social Theory and Social Structure*, pp. 136–139, 166–170, 426–427; Williams, *American Society*, pp. 417–424.

39. Richard Centers, *The Psychology of Social Classes: A Study of Class Consciousness* (Princeton University Press, 1949), p. 148. There was some class differentiation in this expression of confidence: 95 percent for the middle class, and 84 percent for the working class.

40. *Ibid.*, p. 150. Probably some who did not feel they had a good chance to get ahead had already gotten ahead.

41. Barber, *Social Stratification*, p. 345; Lynd and Lynd, *Middletown in Transition*, pp. 13–26, 408–409, 470–476.

42. Kahl, *The American Class Structure*, p. 272. For his data and reasoning, see all of Ch. 9.

43. Barber, *Social Stratification*, pp. 334 ff., and especially pp. 427–477.

44. *Ibid.*, p. 429.

45. See my dissertation, pp. 232–234.

46. Reissman, *Class in American Society*, p. 332.

47. *Ibid.*, p. 299. See also Mills, *White Collar*, pp. 244–248, 265–272.

48. Talcott Parsons, "General Theory in Sociology," in Robert K. Merton, Leonard Broom, and Leonard S. Cottrell, Jr., eds., *Sociology Today: Problems and Prospects* (Basic Books, Inc., 1959), pp. 29–36.

49. James S. Coleman, "The Adolescent Subculture and Academic Achievement," *American Journal of Sociology*, Vol. 65 (January, 1960), pp. 337–347.

50. See *The Annals of the American Academy of Political and Social Science*, Vol. 338 (November, 1961). The entire issue is devoted to "Teen-Age Culture."

51. Herbert H. Hyman, "The Value Systems of Different Classes: A Social Psychological Contribution to the Analysis of Stratification," in Bendix and Lipset, eds., *Class, Status, and Power*, pp. 426–442; Barber, *Social Stratification*, pp. 307–317.

52. A study of the career aspirations of 202 workers on an automobile assembly line who had been employed for twelve years or more revealed that, in general, though they had little expectation of advancement in the plant, disliked the work, and would have preferred better jobs, they were unwilling to quit because they feared loss of pension rights, lower wages, and loss of seniority (in time of recession, the most recently hired are laid off first). Robert H. Guest, "Work Careers and Aspirations of Automobile Workers," *American Sociological Review*, Vol. 19 (April, 1954), pp. 155–163. See also Ely Chinoy, *Automobile Workers and the American Dream* (Doubleday & Company, Inc., 1955).

53. Peter H. Rossi, "The Organizational Structure of an American Community," in Etzioni, ed., *Complex Organizations*, pp. 301–312.

54. Sills, *The Volunteers*, pp. 89–96.

55. Llewellyn Gross and Orville Gursslin, "Middle-Class and Lower-Class Beliefs and Values: A Heuristic Model," in Gouldner and Gouldner, eds., *Modern Sociology*, pp. 168–177.

56. August de B. Hollingshead, *Elmtown's Youth* (John Wiley and Sons, Inc., 1949), Ch. 9.

Chapter 9. CAN THE SOCIAL PRESSURES AGAINST SOCIAL ACTION BE OVERCOME?

1. An enormous range of literature on such topics as democracy and citizenship gives expression to this liberalism. See, e.g., Saul D. Alinsky, *Reveille for Radicals* (The University of Chicago Press, 1946); Arthur M. Schlesinger, Jr., *The Vital Center: The Politics of Freedom* (Houghton Mifflin Company, 1949); Goodwin Watson, *Action for Unity* (Harper & Brothers, 1947).

2. See Peter L. Berger, *Invitation to Sociology: A Humanistic Perspective* (Anchor Books, Doubleday & Company, Inc., 1963), pp. 142–144.